TO
LIVE
AGAIN

TO LIVE AGAIN

Ana Maria Trenchi de Bottazzi

DODD, MEAD & COMPANY
New York

1 2 3 4 5 6 7 8 9 10

Library of Congress Cataloging in Publication Data

De Bottazzi, Ana Maria Trenchi.
    To live again.

    1. De Bottazzi, Ana Maria Trenchi. 2. Pianists—
Biography. I. Title.
ML417.D3A3   786.1'092'4 [B]   78–5029
ISBN 0–396–07570–3

To my mother, ANA SIEIRO DE TRENCHI,
and to the memory of my father, RAUL TRENCHI;
and with thanks to LARRY LORIMER
for his help along the way

Lo que nosotros somos es el regalo de Dios,
en lo que nos convertimos es nuestro regalo a Dios.

What we are is God's gift to us;
what we become is our gift to God.

TO
LIVE
AGAIN

1

NOVEMBER 9, 1974. As I awaken I remember what day this is—perhaps the most important in my life. My stomach ties up in knots. This afternoon at two o'clock I will walk out onto the stage of Town Hall in New York City and sit down at a piano to play my debut recital in the world's music capital.

To people who aren't in music, the importance and seriousness of a New York recital may be hard to understand. Town Hall is a small auditorium near Times Square. Some of the world's greatest performers have appeared there; it is also a traditional place for pianists, singers and other soloists to make their New York debuts. Within a short distance are Carnegie Hall, the Metropolitan Opera House, Avery Fisher Hall (home of the New York Philharmonic orchestra) and half a dozen other musical landmarks. But the most important step toward playing in these more famous places is playing well at that first Town Hall recital. An enthusiastic New York audience and, above all, a good review in the New York *Times* can open doors to a performing career. A flat audience and a bad review will usually end a soloist's plans of ever playing in the great concert halls of the world.

The competition is tremendous. Some weeks during the musical season there may be six or eight pianists appearing for the first time in New York. The majority of them are young, some are very gifted. But few make any particular stir and most are never heard of again.

Unlike the large proportion of debut performers, I am no longer young. By the time I was 23 I had appeared in major recitals and solo performances all over Europe, Africa, Central and South America. The critics said I showed great promise. I had reserved a date at Town Hall for my debut recital in 1962 as a next step to becoming a major international performer. But something happened to me before I could play that engagement, an accident making it seem impossible that I would ever appear there. My doctor had advised me never to attempt such a thing. Now it was twelve years later, and in a few hours I would try to prove the doctor wrong.

I sat down to breakfast and picked at my food. The last week had been a nightmare. My practice for the recital had gone very badly, and my teacher and friend Martin Canin had advised me to cancel the performance altogether. The piano at Town Hall was not the best in the world, yet I couldn't afford the fees to rent or borrow another. Ticket sales had been slow. And all week I had been teaching eight hours a day to help pay for the hall. I had been cross and irritable with Bruno, my husband, and our two children. There had been moments when I wondered if the recital was worth so much grief.

Through the twelve years between my canceled date and this one, appearing in Town Hall had taken on a special meaning for me. I saw it as a new beginning to my career as a performer, a career I had been preparing for since I was three or four years old. All my life people had said, "She is a born musician," and as I grew older music became my first language, a way of expressing myself fully. In the years since the accident my life had been incomplete. I felt that God's plans for me had never been changed, they had only been postponed, and that was why I felt driven to play even against the advice of doctors and teachers. None of them could know how important this recital was.

I dressed hurriedly and Bruno drove me to the beauty parlor right after breakfast. Our home in Centereach, New York, was about a 3 ninety minute ride from Town Hall, so I had to get ready early. I dreaded having my hair done because it still caused me pain.

The accident had not left any lasting marks that were visible. My hands, so precious to a pianist, were untouched. I had no limp and no apparent scars. But inside my head, some of the delicate connections of the brain had been damaged. The injury had affected two things as valuable to a pianist as the hands: coordination and memory. And it had brought on a life of recurring pain—headaches that could turn the most beautiful day into a nightmare. For some reason the hairdryer at the beauty parlor always gave me a headache and caused me to feel sleepy for three or four hours. This was not exactly what I needed on the day of my big performance, but a performer must look attractive as well as play well.

By ten o'clock, Bruno and I were in our car and on the way to Town Hall. We had met and married in Argentina nearly four years after the accident. Bruno is a musician too, and for all the years of our marriage he had been both my greatest support and my firmest critic. We had shared good times and bad times; and we also shared the secret of my handicaps. Only he and my mother knew that my neurologist had advised me never to play again in public. I had not told anyone else, not even my teacher, because I didn't want people to feel sorry for me. If I was to succeed as a pianist, it would be on my own like anyone else, not because of someone's pity or charity.

As we drove toward New York City, I thought back on the discouragements Bruno and I had lived through together. Although we had both grown up in wealthy families, we had learned what it was like to be poor and unemployed. We had seen illness and pain. But we had also had the satisfaction of overcoming our disappointments one at a time, the happiness of two healthy children, the pleasure of friends in our adopted country. If I could play well today, the recital would be another big victory for us.

When we arrived at the hall, I went onstage to warm up. There were still two hours before concert time. I ran through the opening measures of Beethoven's "Appassionata" Sonata, the first selection on the program. I had first learned the piece when I was twelve years old, and had played it in recital in many parts of the world. My mother taught it to me in our home in Buenos Aires and I had studied it with my most influential teacher, Germaine Pinault, in Paris. I remembered struggling to relearn it after the accident on a small upright piano in a private home in Tokyo. But in many ways I would be playing it today for the 5 first time. Never before had it meant so much, never would the reaction of the audience and the critics be so important.

I had in my mind a picture of each page of the sonata, and as I played, I relied on my vision of those pages. Since the accident that was the only way I could remember music. I could not depend on my ear to tell me what came next. If my mental picture of the notes disappeared, I would clatter to a halt without the vaguest idea of what came next. This horrible experience had happened to me in lesser recitals, and I knew it could occur again at any time. But please, Lord, not today.

Just as I was getting to feel comfortable with the piano, the piano tuner arrived to make pre-recital adjustments. So Bruno and I went out to have some lunch. As I had done before every performance of my life, I ordered a steak. Like athletes in training, pianists need energy, and they generally eat well a few hours before a public appearance. Today, however, I was too nervous. There were too many things that might go wrong, and I couldn't help worrying over them. I ate only a little, then gave up. I knew that back at Town Hall I had a box of my favorite chocolates. And I could eat those for last-minute energy.

6   Now there is only a half hour to go. I change

into my concert dress, but every passing moment I get more nervous. Always at such times I have fantasies of running away, of simply disappearing on an airplane while the people in the hall are waiting for me to play.

Martin Canin, my teacher for the past three years, arrives in the waiting room and breaks the spell. Even though he advised me to cancel the recital only a week ago, he is now warm and reassuring. I want to please the audience and the critics, but I especially want to please him. The concert manager arrives. I give him a check—the balance due for his services and rental of the hall. Beginning performers pay their own way (and the tickets sold won't cover half the expenses). The manager says that I should begin in fifteen minutes—ten minutes after the scheduled starting time. Then he adds, "Play as well as you look beautiful." Martin Canin leaves to take his seat in the audience.

I sit down to wait, striving for calm. I take two pain pills as I do before every performance since the accident to guard against a sudden incapacitating headache. These last few minutes of reflection are most important to me. My friend Beverly Rummel, who has stood by all week and came today to help me dress, is the only other person in the room.

Suddenly there is a loud knock on the door. 7

I jump. It's too early, I think. Beverly answers and our friend Bernie Hahnke hurries in with a message from the manager: I must go on at once. I protest; there are still ten minutes left. But Bernie reports that a critic from the New York *Times* has just taken his seat. The manager says this particular critic is an impatient man and will be irritated if the recital doesn't start on the dot. I am hurried to the wings still protesting, and through the stage door I see the piano brightly lit. Feeling rushed, I stand, trying to compose myself for the long walk out to the bench.

At last the moment has come. Twelve years late—twelve years of pain and struggle and doubt—I am appearing for the first time in New York. The next two hours will determine my chance to live again.

2

BRUSSELS, December 7, 1961. I woke up late and the winter sun was streaming in my hotel window. I got out of bed singing. What a wonderful day, I thought. The first time in months that I have been really free.

The night before I had played the last recital in a tour of Europe that had taken me to eight different countries in eight weeks. I had worked on the program for months, perfecting each phrase, polishing each detail. My appearances had all been successful, some even big hits. I was becoming known as a pianist of promise. "She plays so strongly," people said, "and with such a beautiful tone."

At 23 I was already a veteran. I had first appeared in public when I was four, and by the time I was ten I was a regular performer in concert and on the radio. At thirteen I left my home in Argentina to go to Paris for further schooling. At eighteen I returned to Buenos Aires and completed six years of study in two at the university, receiving two advanced 9 music degrees. And ever since, I had been traveling the world, playing, playing and playing.

But now the pressure was off—at least for a few weeks. Here I was in a luxurious hotel. I had nothing to do today except drive back to Paris—back to friends and good times and two weeks of relaxation. It would be one of the few vacations I'd ever had.

I ate an unhurried breakfast, trying to get used to my new leisure. It's funny: when a concert tour begins you can't wait to play each night. But by the time it's half over, you can't wait to be finished. And then when it's all over, it takes you a few days to learn what to do with yourself.

Before I left Brussels I took my car to be serviced. It was a beautiful white Fiat, nearly new—my one prize possession. Since I had gone to Paris as a teenager I had never stayed very long anywhere, so I didn't have a place to call home. But the car I could take with me. That morning there would be time for it to be worked on, then in the afternoon I would drive to Paris.

After leaving the garage, I wandered through the streets. It was cold, but the sun shone brightly. I looked into shop windows, stopped for a light lunch, bought a few small things to please myself. I was still

10

tense—it would take a while to unwind after the weeks of pressure.

Finally the car was ready at 3:30. The roads to Paris weren't very good and soon it would be getting dark, but I wasn't worried. I was a fast driver, and with a little luck I would be there in time for a late dinner. When people asked me what my hobby was, I would reply, "Collecting speeding tickets," and laugh. My friends scolded me for doing everything too fast—eating, playing the piano, talking. But how could anyone resist the excitement of speed in a car?

Driving out of Brussels, I took off my sweater and put it on the seat beside me, turned on the heater and put the radio up loud. Soon I was singing along with Beethoven's "Hammerklavier" Sonata, as the road to Paris sped under the wheels. I thought of Mme. Suzanne Roche, with whom I would be staying in Paris and celebrating my new freedom. Although I had never studied with her, she is one of the world's great piano teachers, and she would appreciate both the success of my tour and my relief that it was over.

Half an hour out of Brussels, as I was approaching the smaller city of Mons, the highway was blocked off by a large sign:

The main road was closed for repairs and all traffic had to take a detour through the outskirts of the city. It was dusk now, and what few cars I saw had their lights on. The radio was playing Chopin's Ballade No. 4, a piece that I had never learned. As I listened, I thought of my approaching recital in New York, my debut in America. The Ballade was so beautiful; I would learn it and play it in Town Hall. I would study the piece as soon as I got to Paris. Even on vacation, I played the piano for fun.

The city of Mons was now passing on my left. I began wondering when the detour would rejoin the main road. I turned off at an intersection to look for the highway. The street was straight and level. As far ahead as I could see there was not another car, so I put the accelerator down to the floor, shifting only when the engine seemed ready to explode. By the time I reached fourth gear, the speedometer showed 145 kilometers (about 90 miles per hour). The speed, the freedom, the soaring music, thoughts of my future—everything made me want to cry out with happiness.

Then I looked up. About three blocks ahead was a huge truck, stopped, in the middle of the road. "Oh no," I remember thinking, but there was no time to be frightened.

To this day I remember every thought and

action as I flew toward that truck.

There was no room to pass on either side. Both sides of the street were lined with tall sturdy trees. Instinctively I jammed my foot down on the brake, but nothing happened! (The road was a sheet of ice, I heard later, and the truck was stopped to spread salt.) I turned the steering wheel sharp to the left, and the car began to skid out of control. Then I turned to the right, as the truck loomed up just ahead of me. I shifted down into lower gears, then into reverse. Still no response. There was going to be a terrible crash, and I had only split-seconds to get ready.

I put my hands on the steering wheel to brace myself for the collision. Suddenly it occurred to me that if I held them there, they would be shattered. I knew I was going to die, but if I had one small chance to live, I would need my hands to play. So I put them in my lap, relaxed and closed my eyes.

How to describe the crash? The grinding sound, the pain as my body flew out of the seat and my head smashed against the steering wheel. A brief impression of my beautiful car closed up like an accordion around me. Smoke and flame. (I was still conscious enough to reach down and turn off the ignition.) The sudden silence when all had come to rest. The taste of blood in my mouth.   13

I reached up to feel my teeth. They seemed to point crazily in different directions. I looked around and there was blood all over. Then I felt faint. I reached for the door handle and pulled. By a stroke of luck, it wasn't damaged. The door swung open and I fell out onto the ice. I was unconscious before I hit the road.

Later I learned that people came running from nearby houses and put blankets over me right where I lay. The ambulance was delayed because a few minutes earlier there had been another accident only a hundred yards down the highway. The driver of that car had died on the way to the hospital. The same ambulance was then sent back to pick me up.

When I regained consciousness, I was in an operating room and a doctor was working on my knee. Thank God, I thought, I'm alive! I lifted my hands and looked at them. They were untouched.

The next morning, the hospital director came to see me. Besides cuts and bruises, I had some internal injuries and my face was so swollen that I looked like a monster. But he reported that by a miracle I had not only survived, but survived without permanent damage. He said I would be able to leave the hospital in about two weeks. Then I could go back to Paris.

I had another visitor that first day—the Argentine ambassador to Belgium. He had heard of the accident on the news and came to see me because I was an Argentine citizen. He asked if he should call my parents and I begged him please not to. I was sure they didn't know about the accident and I knew it would scare them. As soon as I was better, I would call them myself.

Five days later I learned that my mother had known of the accident almost the moment it happened. At the time of the accident—a spring morning in Buenos Aires—she was attending commencement exercises at one of the schools at which she taught. Suddenly she became very nervous and tense. She had trouble getting her breath; she couldn't sit still. Finally she went to the principal and asked to be excused. She didn't know exactly why she felt so apprehensive, but she knew that something terrible had happened to someone she loved. Shortly after returning home, the telephone rang. It was one of her brothers. He asked if she knew where I was that day. She told him that I had just been in Brussels and that I would probably be on my way back to Paris. Then my uncle told her that he had heard on the news that I had been badly injured in an auto accident in Belgium.

For the next five days my family was crazy with worry. One report even said my leg had been amputated. They called the news agencies, but could get no details, not even the town in which I was hospitalized. They did everything except the one thing that would have informed them. Finally, on the fifth day, a cousin suggested they call the Argentine ambassador to Belgium. They then realized how foolish they had been and within a few minutes were talking to me at the hospital.

Fortunately I had good news to report to them. Of course I looked terrible. The right side of my face was horribly swollen and discolored, my mouth was filled with braces to hold the loosened teeth and I was still vomiting blood; but I was apparently on the mend. Two weeks after the accident, just as the doctor had said, I was on a train to Paris.

3

WHEN Mme. Roche met me at the train station she was full of questions about the accident and my condition. I, on the other hand, could scarcely wait to get to her apartment to play the piano. I hadn't touched a keyboard in two weeks—as long as I had gone since I was a child. Music was not just a hobby or way of making a living for me, it was an absolute necessity.

Though I still didn't feel particularly well, I began practicing again from the very first day. It was frustrating to be able to play for only a little while at a time, but the doctors had assured me I would soon get better, so I tried not to worry. But I didn't get better. Instead, I got worse.

First I had trouble with my right eye. The swelling on that side of my face had gone down by now, but the eye didn't work properly. I remember sitting at the keyboard staring helplessly at the music for Albeniz' "Triana." The notes seemed to run together 17 and I couldn't make sense of them. Finally I discovered that if I closed my right eye, the left one saw well enough for me to begin learning the piece.

But then came the headaches. They had begun when I was still in the hospital, although now they'd grown worse. If they came in the middle of a conversation, I would sit there in a daze. If they came when I was at the piano, I just had to put my hands down and wait for them to pass. It felt as if my head was splitting wide open, and I didn't know how to stop them.

One day when I sat down to play, the melody in the right hand became garbled. I stopped and tried the right hand alone. But my arm felt heavy and the fingers would not perform unless I concentrated on every single move. About the same time I began having trouble walking even though my knee was almost well. My right leg, too, felt heavy and wouldn't obey. Sometimes the arm and leg would work, but then they'd get heavy again. I never knew if I could trust them.

One night early in January I woke up at 2 A.M. wanting to scream. I thought I was going to explode. I stumbled into the bathroom, taking care not to wake Mme. Roche, turned on the cold water faucet and put my head in the basin. For half an hour I stood there with the cold water running from the back of my neck down through my hair—it was the only relief I could find.

The agony returned every night for a week. Then one night Mme. Roche woke up and found me running cold water on my head. She was frantic. She urged me to call a doctor. But I had very little money—most of it went to the hospital in Mons. My father in Argentina was a millionaire, but we'd had a bitter argument a few months earlier. I was still angry at him and it seemed better to die than to ask him for help. So I told Mme. Roche to wait a few days, praying things would get better.

They didn't. Every evening the headaches came with greater force. I lay in the middle of Mme. Roche's living room while she applied ice to my neck, my forehead, my temples. She knew this couldn't go on much longer, and so did I.

Mme. Roche got the name of the best neurologist in Paris and called to make an appointment for me. But the doctor's secretary announced that the next appointment was in July, six months away.

Mme. Roche said this was an emergency. She described my symptoms and asked for an early appointment. But the secretary would not give in. Did Mme. Roche want the appointment in July or not?

Mme. Roche raised her voice. If I didn't get an appointment, she said, I was going to die and she would then let the whole city know that Dr. Rivadeau-Duma had turned away a dying patient. The secretary paused, consulted the doctor, then told Mme. Roche the doctor would make a very special exception and see me at five o'clock that evening—after regular office hours. Before she hung up, the nurse said, "Your friend better be dying."

By now, I was spending more and more time each day in bed, in too much pain to do anything else. But that afternoon at four, I got up, put on some make-up to cover the remaining bruises on my face and picked out my handsomest dress. All my life I had been taught to look my best. Then I took a taxi to the doctor's office.

I was met by his secretary. She looked at me as if to say, "So you're the one who's making all the noise." Then she showed me to an examining room and left for the day.

Numb and a little scared, I sat waiting for the doctor. For the first time I let myself think how serious all this might be. Something was very wrong, and I was afraid to find out just what. But if the doctor could only help make the headaches go away, that would be enough.

20   Minutes later, Dr. Rivadeau-Duma ap-

peared. He was a tall, slender man in his early sixties who looked at me for a moment and then looked all around the room. When he saw that I was the only one there, he said, "I hope you are not the patient who said she was dying."

I swallowed and replied softly, "Yes, Doctor, I am."

Suddenly he was furious. "You keep me here after a long day of work," he said, his voice rising, "and you are just another spoiled young girl who thinks the world turns on your little aches and pains. I should throw you out of here."

As he went on and on, I sat there feeling smaller and smaller. All my life I had been brought up to please older people—my mother, who sat next to me at the piano while I practiced, day after day; my father, whose rages I had learned to fear; my teacher for five years in Paris, Mlle. Pinault, who always saw what was wrong with my playing and never mentioned what was right. Now this distinguished old doctor was scolding me for not being sick.

"Please, God," I thought, "let there be something the matter."

Finally the doctor agreed to examine me and asked what was wrong. I told him about the accident and my stay in the hospital at 21

Mons. Then I described the headaches. For the next hour, he said nothing except to ask me to do this or to do that.

I don't remember all the details of the examination, except that in the first few minutes he took his little hammer and tried to check my reflexes. No matter how hard he tried, he couldn't find any. I didn't realize then that this might point to serious brain damage, but I saw the doctor was becoming very preoccupied. "Thank God," I thought. "He has found something really wrong."

An hour later he finished his examination and invited me into his office. He was a completely different person. He smiled and spoke in a soothing voice. "I must really be sick," I thought.

Now he asked me to describe the accident —everything I remembered about it. When I came to the last seconds before the crash and told him that I had intentionally put my hands in my lap to protect them from injury, the doctor muttered, "What do you call a donkey in Spanish?"

"Burro," I answered, surprised at the question.

"Only a burro would be stupid enought to choose to break his head rather than his hands," he said. This seemed an odd remark
to me. For if he knew anything about pianists,

he would know that we all go to any lengths to protect our hands.

Then he asked if I was losing liquid from my nose. Yes, I said, and I couldn't understand why since I didn't have a cold. He examined the liquid. "Just as I suspected," he said quietly. "You have meningitis, too."

Then he tried to explain my condition to me. I don't know how much I understood at the time. My head was aching and I was tired from the long examination. He said my skull had been fractured—shattered, really—in the accident. The liquid from my nose was the fluid that normally surrounds and protects the brain. Because of the break in the fluid sac I had contracted meningitis, an often fatal infection of the brain lining.

My failing sight and the creeping paralysis in my right arm and leg were caused by blood clots that were pressing down on the part of the brain that controlled the right side of my body. He told me that if I didn't receive medical attention immediately I would die within 48 hours. It was worse than I had allowed myself to think.

The reason the doctor in Mons had not discovered this trouble was because my external injuries masked the internal ones. My right knee had been badly jammed, so no one could test it for reflexes, and my right eye was swol- 23 len shut for weeks, so it would have been difficult to detect any problem there. And if I had suffered damage to the right side of my brain, there would have been paralysis on the *left* side of my body. Who would have guessed that blood clots were pressing in on the *left* side of my brain?

Finally, the doctor in Mons had acted very strangely. He used to visit my room and stare at me for minutes at a time. Then, as if coming back to life, he would say, "You were very very lucky," and leave the room. I later learned that just the week before my accident his only son, who was about to become a doctor himself, had been killed in an auto accident. So this man might not have recognized my symptoms even if they had been easy to see.

Well, what was to be done? Dr. Rivadeau-Duma wanted to admit me to the hospital immediately. But all I could think of were the many reasons why I could not receive treatment now. I had no money and no insurance, I said, so there was no way for me to enter the hospital.

The doctor asked about my parents. Could they afford to help? I was very tired at the time and in no mood to lie. I admitted that my father was a wealthy man in Argentina, but then added that we were not on good terms;

I could *not* ask him for money. Was there any-one else?

"No," I said. "Let's just forget the whole thing."

I still don't understand what made me re-fuse to ask for help with death so near. I knew my father loved me more than anyone in the world and that he would help me no matter how angry he was. But at that moment it seemed better to die than to ask.

Now Dr. Rivadeau-Duma was angry again. To please him, I promised that if he would let me go home, I would call him later in the evening to make arrangements. But I was lying.

For his records, however, he asked me the name and address of the person I was staying with in Paris as well as my father's name and address in Argentina. Then I paid him what money I had for the examination, put my coat on and let myself out. It was 6:30 and the streets were dark.

4

WHEN you are alive and well, death seems a terrible prospect. But as I left the doctor's office, I was looking it right in the face and it didn't seem so terrible at all.

"Well, this is it," I remember thinking. "There is no money for treatment, so I suppose you'll die." I felt sorry for my father and mother because I knew they would miss me. But few others would care. My first thought was how to use the little time I had left.

Paris was my second home. I had first travelled there at thirteen and had spent most of every year there until I was eighteen. Then a few years later, when I began touring, I returned often to visit friends and to enjoy the city itself. Now on this chilly winter evening I wanted to see it once more.

Walking the streets with the cold air in my face, I seemed to notice everything around me —the bright lights, the sounds, the people— down to the smallest detail. With so little time

left it all seemed so precious.

The doctor's office was not far from L'E-toile, the broad avenue that makes its way to the Arc de Triomphe. I followed it all the way, then walked down the Champs Elysees. Wherever I looked I was reminded of my earlier days here—of something I bought at this store, of the day I ate at that cafe. Soon I came to the church of La Madeleine. I stopped and looked at it, remembering the many times Mother and I had gone there to Mass. I thought of Monsignor Franceschi, a family friend who had travelled with us to Paris on our very first trip. I had loved him and wondered what he would advise me to do now. Was he perhaps watching me at that very moment?

When I finally left the front of the church, I was stiff and it was hard to walk. But a few blocks later I forgot my body, lost once again in my memories. Past the St. Lazaire Station and through familiar streets I went until I came to 31 Rue de Rocher. Looking up I could see the windows of the apartment where I had lived with my mother and brother when we first came to Paris. So many things had happened in that apartment—both happy and sad —but now I remembered just one.

In Argentina, a girl's fifteenth birthday is a special occasion. It is her coming of age. As my fifteenth birthday approached, the big ques- 27 tion was whether my father would come from Buenos Aires to celebrate it with us. He and I had always been close. In fact, he would call me four or five times a day from the office when I was at home. And when he returned from his club at night he would come up to see me last thing before my bedtime.

It was not a matter of money—he could travel to Paris whenever he wanted. But he was a busy man, and the question was whether he had time to make the long trip from South America. Each week when he called I asked if he was coming. But all he said was that he would have to see.

The week before my birthday he called and said that he was sending a gift with a business associate. The man would arrive on the night before my birthday and we were to pick him up at the airport. I was overjoyed because I knew (or thought I knew) that the "business associate" would be father himself. All week I got more and more excited. Then just two days before he was to come, the long-distance operator called from Buenos Aires and said, "On Thursday [the day of my birthday] I shall have a call from Senor Raul Trenchi. Will you be at home to accept it?" All at once my world fell through. He wasn't coming after all. I was heartbroken.

On Wednesday night, we asked a friend to

meet the man at the airport. My mother, brother and I sat up waiting for him to drop off the gift. After a special dinner, we played cards, just waiting for my father's associate to come so that we could go to bed.

At eleven o'clock the doorbell rang and I went to answer it. I was looking down at the man's shoes when I suddenly noticed his briefcase and realized that the "man" was my father! I screamed loud enough to wake half of Paris and jumped into his arms. It was the happiest birthday surprise of my life.

Now I stood outside the building where all that had taken place, crying. I was cold and tired and wanted so badly to talk to him. I didn't care about my health or about money for my care. I just needed him to put his arms around me so that nothing terrible would happen. . . . But at the same time I knew that couldn't be. Our anger at each other had been growing over the months. He had moved out of our house and was living his own life now. I hated his new life and wanted him back. He was angry that I begrudged him his freedom. We both were strong-willed and ugly when we were mad. If I called him, the subject of my health would come up, then the operation and what it would cost. It would seem I was calling for money. And I would not do that.

A few blocks away, on the Rue de Madrid 29

was the National Conservatory of Music where I had studied during my Paris years. And across the street was the Argentine consulate where I had spent many afternoons when I was homesick, reading Argentine newspapers and magazines.

As I walked back past the St. Lazaire Station and on toward the Paris Opera, I suddenly realized that it was ten o'clock. I had been walking for three and a half hours without a thing to eat. I went to a bar near the Opera for a snack. But that stop nearly finished me. I was exhausted. It was time to return to Mme. Roche's and sleep—even if I was going to die tomorrow.

I took a bus back across the city.

The door of the apartment burst open and I was surrounded by people.

"Where have you been?"

"Thank God she's here!"

"We thought you were dead!"

At first I didn't understand what they were talking about. Their chatter didn't make any sense until Mme. Roche explained everything.

Dr. Rivadeau-Duma had made good use of the names and addresses I had given him. He had called the Argentine embassy and explained the situation, asking the Ambassador if he could reach my father to see if he would pay for my treatment. A few minutes later my father called Dr. Rivadeau-Duma directly and said that he would pay whatever the best treatment cost. Then the doctor had called Mme. Roche and told her of my dangerous condition. I should be put to bed as soon as I got home and the ambulance would come to take me to the hospital.

There was only one problem—where was I? I was hiking through Paris on this midwinter night unaware that all of my friends and the Paris police were frantically looking for me. Many of them thought I must have collapsed and died before reaching home.

Within minutes after I arrived at Mme. Roche's I was on the way to a neurological hospital in Neuilly, a suburb of Paris. Soon after I reached my room, Dr. Rivadeau-Duma arrived. He had heard of my evening's activities and he greeted me gruffly.

"Bon soir, burro," he said.

5

MY ROOM at the neurosurgical hospital was beautiful and expensive. Actually, it was more a suite. In addition to the room where I lay in bed, there was a full bathroom made of translucent bricks and a sitting area for visitors.

The doctors dared not operate until my meningitis had been controlled. So for the first week I lay motionless while they gave me medication and took endless X rays to prepare for the operation. They would take one X ray, move the camera a fraction of an inch, take another, and so on for hours at a time. My headaches continued. But when I was lying in bed they came less often, and when they did come the pain could be controlled with medication. There was some lingering paralysis in my right arm and leg, and the vision in my right eye was still imperfect. In addition, I began to have trouble speaking and understanding the conversation of others.

32   I was restless. Every day was just like the

one before, and it began to seem that nothing would ever happen. I began telling people that I wanted to play the piano. Everyone was kind, but they all said, "As soon as you are better, dear." No one seemed to realize how important playing was to me.

The second week of my stay, I decided I could not stand it any longer. I decided to escape—leave the hospital long enough to find a piano. I made my plans carefully. First I borrowed money from a friend who came to visit, saying that I wanted to tip one of the private nurses who were at my bedside twenty-four hours. I began to watch to see when I might slip away most easily.

At eight o'clock in the evening of the tenth day, I asked my nurse for some ice water—knowing that she would have to go all the way to the kitchen for the ice. As soon as she left my room with the glass, I jumped out of bed, put on some shoes and a coat and walked out into the hall. Although the paralysis in my right leg gave me a limp, I made every effort to walk normally.

I had to wait in the hallway for an elevator, but one came quickly and it was empty. On the ground floor I simply strolled past the main desk and through the front door. It was cold outside and by this time I felt dizzy and faint. But still I walked as fast as I could away 33 from the hospital, afraid that at any moment a group of doctors or nurses would come running after me. Once I was out of sight of the hospital I hailed a taxi and gave the driver Mme. Roche's address—but I asked him to go the long way around so I could retrace the path of my earlier walk through the city less than two weeks before.

About an hour later we pulled up in front of Mme. Roche's. She was waiting for me. The hospital had called her, of course, to say that I had left.

"What are you doing here?" she shouted. "Are you crazy? What is the matter with you?" When I told her that I just wanted to play the piano for a few minutes, she was so surprised that she agreed to wait 30 minutes before calling the ambulance. As a musician, she could understand my need to play. I've often wondered what I sounded like that night. Nor do I remember what was going through my mind.

When the ambulance brought me back to the hospital, everyone was upset. Dr. Rivadeau-Duma was so furious he didn't even call me "burro." At the time I couldn't understand their anger. But I do now.

Almost immediately my condition began to deteriorate. Within a couple of days my right side was completely paralyzed and I was blind in my right eye. Even worse, I "lost" three of my four languages—not being able either to speak or to understand them. One of these was Spanish, my own mother tongue! The only language left to me now, for some reason, was French.

At about this time Mother arrived from Buenos Aires. When she came to my bedside, she spoke Spanish, and I couldn't understand her. She was even more shocked when she realized I didn't recognize her.

"I am your mother," she finally said in French. But I told her she couldn't be. My mother is in Argentina, I said.

The last few days before the operation are a haze, and I don't remember them in any order. One day the surgeon who was to operate came in to get my signature on a paper granting permission for the operation. I asked him what he was going to do to me.

"Oh, we're just going to fix something in your forehead," he said. "It shouldn't take half an hour."

Then one morning they came and gave me some anesthetic and began wheeling me up to the operating room. On the way, I saw Mother (although she wasn't my mother to me) and some other friends in the waiting room. They were crying. She came over and kissed me. When we got to the waiting room a nurse began to shave my head.

"Why are you shaving my whole head if you're only going to fix my forehead?" I asked the surgeon. He got a funny look on his face and gave a nurse a signal to give me some more anesthetic.

As I drifted off I remember thinking, "Here we go again . . . he didn't tell me the truth. . . ."

The operation was on a Monday. When I woke up it was Friday. I was lying on my back on a perfectly flat bed in a dark room. A nurse was standing beside me, and her first words were, "Don't move your head."

Then my mother came in and I knew immediately who she was. She spoke to me in Spanish and I answered in Spanish. I also learned that day that I could move my right arm and leg again—the paralysis was gone.

All these were good signs. But the doctors wouldn't know for weeks how successful the operation had been. Of course the operation hadn't taken half an hour as the doctor had suggested. It had taken ten hours. The surgeons had cleared out all the chips from my shattered skull and removed fifteen blood clots from the surface of the brain. It was the clots that had been putting pressure on the

brain, causing my headaches, paralysis and

other problems. Then they put a platinum plate in my forehead to take the place of the bone. No matter how carefully an operation of this kind is done, the surgeons must handle and jostle the brain. So no one can be sure of the results until weeks or months later.

For the first three weeks I had to lie motionless on that flat bed in a very dark room to give the brain and the tissues time to heal. After that, I was allowed a tiny pillow and a light shining through the door from the next room. Then a larger pillow and a little more light. After eight weeks I was allowed out of the bed for the first time. And a month or so later I was strong enough to be released from the hospital.

During those months of recuperation, the hospital kept sending neurologists to my room to ask me questions or get me to do some simple thing with an arm or a leg. So many of those tasks seemed foolish. "Touch your nose with your right index finger," one would say. "What year is this?" asked another. "What year were you born?" "Where is your home?" "How much is five and seven?" Often I couldn't do or answer what they asked, but I still thought the questions were silly.

Now I realize they were all testing to see what my mind could do—and what it couldn't do. Had the accident or the operation dam- 37 aged some of the delicate mechanism that allows us to think and reason and remember? The odd part about a brain injury is that no one ever knows for sure just what damage has been done. Everyone knows what a thigh bone or a heart muscle is supposed to do, and if one of them is injured, the injury can be measured. But the brain is so complicated that determining such damage accurately is nearly impossible. And if the person whose brain was injured has a good imagination, he or she may imagine that "ever since that day" he or she hasn't been quite the same.

By the time I could walk around, dress myself and carry on a conversation with a visitor, Mother and I were talking about going home to Argentina. Suddenly I was hopeful again. Spring was in the air in Paris, and for me it had been a long winter.

Finally the day came to check out of the hospital. We planned to fly the next week to Buenos Aires. Dr. Rivadeau-Duma asked that my mother and I come in for one last conference with him before we left. So the day before our departure, we went back to the hospital.

"It is a miracle you are alive," he began, "and it is an even greater miracle that you are nearly normal. You are the same person, you
can remember your life before the accident,

you can reason and feel emotion. But," he continued, "you are not completely cured. There are some disabilities you will probably have for the rest of your life. For one thing you have lost the sense of smell. For another, your memory is impaired in some subtle but important ways. You will never be able to memorize music again, and you may have trouble remembering small details of everyday life. You may also find that your coordination is impaired—that your fingers are not as fast or accurate as they once were. Each of these disabilities will be hardly noticeable to you when you are relaxed. But under pressure or stress they will get worse—your memory will 'lock,' your coordination will falter."

Mother and I looked at each other. What was he leading up to?

"So," he said, "my advice to you is to give up your career as a concert pianist. You are young and pretty and talented. Build yourself a new life—get married, teach the piano, have fun. If you do try to be a concert performer, you will only be asking for bitterness and disappointment."

We thanked him. He had saved my life and been thoughtful to Mother throughout. But as we left I simply couldn't imagine my "new life." From the time I was two I had been training to be a performer. I had devoted more 39 training to be a performer. I had devoted more than half my waking hours to that single goal. Music had become a natural language to me, my way of expressing myself. Why did the doctor think I had saved my hands during the accident or run away from the hospital a few months earlier? Yet now he was asking me to give up, to do something less strenuous, to treat myself like an invalid.

During those few minutes I resolved not to. I was a performing artist and I would continue to be one. Mother and I agreed never to mention the doctor's advice. The musical world was not to look on me with condescension or pity. I would prove the doctor wrong, and no one need know.

In the years that followed, I often went back on my resolution. There were times when a concert career seemed impossibly far away and I would tell myself that I *could* be happy being a good teacher and a good wife and mother. But then someone or something would remind me and I'd begin again. As my mother always said, God had given me the talent and I owed Him a gift in return—not an excuse.

I had no idea how long or how difficult the road back to the concert stage would be. Yet 40 I knew it wasn't impossible, no matter what the doctor had said. The words "I can't" didn't exist in my vocabulary. So with this resolve in mind, I prepared to go back to Buenos Aires and become a pianist once again.

⚜ 6

DURING those long weeks after the operation I had plenty of time to think about my life and reflect on the people who had been important to me. It was fitting that my mother would share the secret of Dr. Rivadeau-Duma's chilling advice, because she was most responsible for what I am. To know her is to know a great deal about me.

My mother, Ana Sieiro de Trenchi, was born of European immigrant parents in Rio de Janeiro but her family soon moved to Buenos Aires. Her father was a Spaniard who wrote many years for the most prestigious newspaper in Argentina. Her mother had grown up in a small town in Italy. As a teenager my grandmother had her heart so set on emigrating that eventually the family agreed to let her go to Argentina with her brother. (When she married my grandfather a few years later, her brother returned to Italy.)

Mother always loved music, and was an
accomplished pianist as a teenager. In addi-

tion, she had her mother's spirit of independence. She concluded that she must go to Paris for advanced study of the piano and carried on a long campaign to get her way. Since it was then unthinkable for a girl of seventeen to travel alone, my grandfather finally agreed to take the whole family to Paris for a year. He obtained a leave of absence from his newspaper and made reservations for the trip.

Just before their scheduled departure, my grandfather did not come home from work one night. Only in the morning did he return —carried in a coffin. He had died of a heart attack while having coffee with his colleagues. The Paris trip was canceled, and Mother was left to help support her family and make do with whatever musical training she could find in Buenos Aires. A few weeks later she took on her first students, and from that day on her main interest has been teaching.

Mother attended the conservatory in Buenos Aires, becoming one of the first women to receive the most advanced degree there. And while still in her early twenties, she organized a music school that within ten years had become one of the most prestigious in South America. In a day when women were excluded from the arts and the professions, her talent for organization was as remarkable as her gift for music.

43

My parents met while Mother was working her hardest with the school and were married a few years later.

Mother tells a strange story about the day I was born. That morning her labor pains began, but she also felt an overwhelming desire to play the piano. So she sat down and played for six hours straight—until only a few minutes before I was born. In all her life, she says, she never played as well as she played that day.

Less than a week later, she took up her teaching again. My crib was always in the room. Even when I was old enough to walk, I stayed in the lesson room most of the time.

One Sunday afternoon when I was two, I was "playing" on the concert grand in the living room. My father, who knew very little about music, was reading the newspaper. He noticed that I wanted to play a scale, but always seemed to hunt for the right note to start on. Not understanding the reason for this, he called Mother and asked why I was doing it.

Mother had prayed from the moment she knew she was expecting that her child would have musical talent, but she had never tested me because she was so afraid of being disappointed. Now she did, however, and was astonished to find that I could name any note she played and even identify three notes when she played them together as a chord. Crying softly, she knelt down and hugged me, repeating over and over, *"Mi hija querida"*—my dearest daughter. The next afternoon my father came home and told me he had brought me something. "Go look from the balcony," he said. I looked and there was an open truck stacked full of toys. He didn't know or like music, but he was so proud of me that he had spent a whole month's salary on gifts for me.

That was the beginning of my musical life. For some days Mother puzzled about how to teach music to a child too young to read. Gradually, however, she arrived at a method that she later wrote down and published. The method has since been used to teach many other young musicians. From the beginning she dreamed that I would grow up to be a great performer, just as she herself had hoped to be before her father died. I played in public for the first time when I was four, and about that same time my father asked my uncle, who was an artist, to paint a picture of me at the piano, a picture that hangs in our living room today.

Shortly after this first recital, my brother was born and for a few weeks I didn't get the three or four little lessons every day from my mother. So I began to practice on my own. One day Mother, sick in bed, heard someone

45

playing Clementi Sonatinas in another room. She asked a maid to see who was in the house practicing. The maid reported that it was me. Sick as she was, Mother got up to see for herself. Once again I had surprised her, this time by playing something she hadn't yet taught me. From then on she set up a regular schedule of lessons after deciding that I should practice two hours a day. This increased to four hours when I was six, to six hours when I was nine and finally to eight hours after I passed twelve.

Musically, my childhood was amazingly rich. I had my mother to teach me, and by the time I was ten we had eleven pianos in our large apartment. Mother took me frequently to the theater, to concerts and to the ballet. Dance soon became my other great interest. I began to take lessons at the Teatro Colon, Argentina's most important dance company, and appeared in child parts in major productions. In fact, as a young girl I wanted to be a dancer more than a pianist.

But when I was twelve, Mother insisted that I choose either the piano or dance. With strong support from her, the piano won out because I didn't dare go against her wishes. But even today I can't bear to watch ballet. I become jealous of the dancers and sad to the
heart.

My childhood was rich in other ways too. By the time I was five, my father had become a wealthy man. He showered me with gifts—there was nothing in the world I couldn't have just for the asking. We lived in a large apartment and my brother and I even had our own private playground on the roof.

Yet for all that, my life was a strange and lonely one. When I was old enough to go to school, my mother decided that a regular school would waste too much of my time and energy. So she hired tutors to teach me privately. I still remember my disappointment at not being able to go to school like my cousins and other "normal" children. A year or two later I persuaded my father to buy me a school outfit (the standard uniform worn then by all schoolchildren in Argentina). When my mother was busy, I would put it on and pretend I was going to school. A few times I even snuck outdoors and walked around, happy to have people think I was just a normal child.

But in reality, my life belonged to Mother. Not only did she keep track of my hours of practice, she supervised my every move. I was almost never allowed to go out of the house unless she or my father were with me. I had no friends my own age and no life outside music and the family. My brother and I were too far apart in age ever to be close, so I never even thought of him as a friend. I longed to run away and see the world, but the best I could do was to fool my governess by reading a comic book while playing monotonous exercises. If I didn't at least pretend to practice, Mother would sit up with me after my bedtime until I had put in the correct number of hours. Once or twice she did this until two or three in the morning. "I know you're not learning anything this late," she said, "but I want it to be a lesson to you that your practicing must always come first."

This routine continued until I was past twelve. The only thing that made it bearable was my close friendship with my father, who didn't know anything about music.

7

A MOST important period of my early life started in December 1950 when I was twelve. For the next two and a half years I would be separated from my father and tied even more closely to Mother. I would meet two people whose influence on me would be stronger than anyone outside my family. And I would suffer great physical and emotional turmoil.

It all started when my father suggested that Mother and I spend part of the South American summer (December through April) on a cruise to Europe and the Middle East. He had read about a luxury tour and thought it a good idea for us to break our routines for a few weeks even though he would be unable to come. Neither Mother nor I had ever been to Europe.

At first she was opposed to the trip. For even though the music school was not in session during the summer, she still had private students. And of course she was reluctant to 49 have me give up my eight hours a day "no matter what" at the piano. But when my father told her that Monsignor Gustavo Franceschi, one of the most important and admired churchmen in South America, would be accompanying the tour she softened a bit. Mother had always been a devout Catholic and had heard much about Monsignor Franceschi. My father suggested that before we decided whether or not to go we should visit the Monsignor and find out more about the tour.

Our meeting with Monsignor Franceschi was love at first sight. A tall, broad-shouldered man in his late sixties with graying hair and a warm smile, he had come to Argentina from France as a boy. During his many years in the church he had become known as both a distinguished scholar and a dedicated priest, yet one who was very sophisticated in the ways of the world. When he learned that I was a pianist, his eyes lit up. He loved music, he said, and had been collecting recordings of pianists for thirty years. And we then talked about music. Even before we left Mother and I had decided to go on the trip if only to become better acquainted with this wonderful man.

One thing still troubled me, however, and 50   that was the necessity of leaving my father. In the past few years he had become my best friend in the world and I was beset by childish fears that something would happen to him while I was gone. When the ship began to move away from the dock, I stood on the deck waving to him and crying harder and harder. By the time I lost sight of him I was hysterical. He had promised to write me every day and to call by ship-to-shore telephone, but nothing was enough. All through the trip I missed him terribly, but at the same time I began to have fun and to form a lasting friendship with the second man in my life—Monsignor Franceschi.

On board ship I had more freedom than I had ever known. I met a girl a few years older than I, and Mother seemed content to let me run loose—with one important exception. There was no way for me to practice eight hours a day, but she still expected me to play an hour or two on a piano in one of the ship's lounges. Within a few days these practice sessions became more like chamber recitals, as passengers would come into the lounge, sit quietly and listen. The most faithful listener of all was the Monsignor. Each day he stayed until I was finished; we then sat and talked about the music. He told Mother that he was amazed at my playing and asked her what plans she had made for my continued training. He knew as well as she that opportunities for advanced study in piano were lacking in Argentina. Anyone who wanted to become a performing musician would have to spend several years in Paris, Vienna or, perhaps, the United States. Since the Monsignor was of French extraction himself, he suggested that Mother consider sending me to Paris. He had no idea then that my mother's fondest dream had been to study in Paris herself. She agreed this would be ideal, but she told the Monsignor that my father would probably never allow me to go.

We arrived in Paris on January 23, and Monsignor Franceschi took us on our first tour of the city. He made a special point to mention things that would interest me because he was still full of the idea that I should study there. From then on Monsignor and I were very close. I called him *abuelito*—Grandfather—and he treated me like a granddaughter. His view of the world was big enough to encompass both the spiritual and the temporal and to see me as both a musician and a human being. For my part, I brought him relief from his heavy daily responsibilities. He always said, "Others bring me their problems, but you bring me only happiness."

Monsignor Franceschi was a serious man, and as the years passed he taught me some important lessons. He never asked me if I went to church or said my prayers, but in our conversations and letters he was always pointing out the difference between honesty and dishonesty, between upright behavior and what is wrong. Six years after the cruise, the Monsignor ran into serious trouble with Juan Peron, the President of Argentina, because he refused to subordinate the church and his own conscience to the dictator. Even though he was past seventy at the time, he spent several months in jail for his actions.

When we returned to Argentina, Monsignor Franceschi began a campaign to persuade my father that I should go to Paris to study. For many months the battle raged, the Monsignor and my mother on one side and Father on the other. Paris finally won. Had it not been for Monsignor Franceschi, I might have lived my whole life in Buenos Aires.

Mother decided to come to Paris with me and hired a temporary director to run her music school. I was never really consulted about the matter since everyone assumed I wanted what they thought was best for me. So it was settled. In September 1952, shortly after my fourteenth birthday, Mother, my brother and I sailed for France. This time, Father and Monsignor Franceschi were both on the dock. I felt scared and very much alone as 53 the ship pulled away; and I continued to wave long after I had lost sight of them.

We knew almost no French when we arrived in Paris and had little else beyond a few introductions to musicians from people we knew in Argentina. But one of these musicians took an immediate personal interest in us. She was Simone Couderc, a principal singer in the Paris Opera. She said that she didn't know much about piano teachers, but she had a very distinguished friend who did, a woman named Germaine Pinault. Mlle. Pinault was to become the fourth person who would have a major influence on my early life —along with Mother, my father and Monsignor Franceschi.

Germaine Pinault was born with a heart defect. All her life she had been warned not to exert herself and advised that she might die suddenly at any moment. In spite of this, she attended the Paris Conservatory and studied with Leschititzky, a leading student and disciple of Franz Liszt. Although she had never performed in public or taken on regular students, she was regarded in Paris musical circles as one of the outstanding pianists of her generation. Among her admirers and friends were Nadia Boulanger, perhaps the most esteemed teacher of music in this century and

Yves Nat, the great French pianist.

When we arrived at Mlle. Pinault's apartment, we found her looking as frail as the doctors told her she was. She weighed barely a hundred pounds, and her arms were matchstick thin. However, we soon learned that Germaine Pinault had not only incredible strengths but a will of iron.

Right at the start she said that she had never taught anyone because of her health and that she would not be able to teach me. After she heard me play she turned to my mother: "Your daughter is a born musician, but her technique is not good enough. Someone must start from the beginning with her and form a new technique or she will never become a great pianist." The best teacher in Paris was Yves Nat, she said, and gave us a letter of recommendation to him even though she warned that he seldom took students as young as I. She was kind and helpful, but firm about her own inability to teach.

Messr. Nat accepted me as a pupil and I enrolled in several classes at the Conservatory including theory, harmony, sightreading and solfege, and German music. These classes, along with practice and preparation made for a full schedule. My routine in Buenos Aires had been simple by comparison.

Then, two weeks after our first meeting with Germaine Pinault, Simone Couderc called. She reported that Mlle. Pinault had been worrying about my situation. She knew that Yves Nat would not be able to devote the necessary time to me, and after much consideration she had decided to offer to teach me herself. Her conditions, however, were severe. She didn't know how long she would live, she said, and so she wanted to accomplish as much as possible with me in a very short time. If I wanted to study with her I would have to come to her apartment five hours a day, seven days a week. No exceptions.

Mother was amazed and a little troubled by the long hours, but she believed this was the chance we had been waiting for. The next day she accepted Mlle. Pinault's offer and her conditions—*in addition* to all my other work. At this stage of my life, however, I did whatever Mother asked me to do, so I began to go to Mlle. Pinault's every day.

I can't imagine anyone working harder than I did that year. In the theory class I was trying to catch up to precocious French students who at the age of ten could already write complex fugues on a set theme. (Only the warmth and concern of our teacher, Mlle. Dieudonne, kept me at it.) The rapid training of my ear and eye in the other courses often kept me busy doing assignments until late at night. Twice a week

I had to be prepared for Messr. Nat. (He didn't

know I was also studying with Germaine Pinault.) And then there were Mlle. Pinault's five-hour lessons each day. Whatever time I had left over I used to practice at home.

Other girls my age, even those at the Conservatory, went to parties, were able to spend an hour in a coffee house or go to an opera or concert. I didn't have time for such things since I was working from seven in the morning to nine or ten at night. Mother, however, was freer than she had ever been. Without the school and her students to worry about, she kept an even closer eye on me. Sometimes I hated her and even wished she would die so that I too could be free. But musically I was growing by leaps and bounds, and being shown how much a person can learn in a short time even against his or her will.

8

AT THE end of my first year in Paris my fifteenth birthday was approaching—a very special anniversary in Argentina. I wanted more than anything for my father to be with me on that important occasion. I have already described my depression when it seemed he wasn't coming and my excitement when he arrived. At that moment there was no one in the world dearer or more necessary to me.

My father, Raul Trenchi, was born to a family of Italian immigrants in Buenos Aires. He was the fourth or fifth of twelve children, and like his brothers he went to work on the docks as soon as he was old enough to leave grade school. But there was something special about him. From the beginning he was more ambitious and energetic than the rest. By the time he reached his mid-twenties he had a responsible job in an import-export firm.

He met Mother at an outdoor dance in a park near the city where she had come with
the parents of one of her students. He asked

her to dance, but he was clumsy and stepped all over her. She never told him her address, but one day shortly thereafter he appeared at her house. They saw each other for a few months, but then Mother said she didn't care to see him any more. And when he went away, she thought that was it.

At the end of the school year, Mother arranged a special gala performance for her students in a big concert hall. The last number was a spectacular piece that gave everyone a chance to participate—instrumentalists, singers and dancers. Just as it concluded, but before the curtain could come down, the audience's applause was interrupted by squeals of delight from the students, who were suddenly scampering about the stage snatching for pieces of candy. When Mother came out to see what was going on, there in the nearest box was my father and two friends throwing down candies by the handful. Both amused and touched, she began to see him again. Four years later they were married.

When I was very young, my father quit his job to go into business for himself. In no time at all his intelligence and energy led to success and to an expensive new hobby—owning and betting on racehorses. Within a few years, however, Father was one of the leading breeders and trainers in Argentina. When I was   59 about twelve, he came home from the track one night very drunk—the only time I ever remember seeing him that way—and in such high spirits that he could not sit still or keep quiet. That day he had entered a big red horse named Hercules in an important race. Since the horse was unknown and inexperienced, it ran at very long odds. My father bet on him and Hercules won, bringing my father more than $100,000. No wonder he was drunk. Shortly thereafter he obtained the exclusive right to import spare parts for all American-made automobiles in Argentina; and since these were about the only cars available in the country at that time, we were soon one of the wealthiest families in South America.

Still, I didn't view my father as a money-maker. Money was almost never a subject of conversation. To me he had become my one good friend in a lonely, overdisciplined exis-tence. As Mother increased her demands for practice time and achievement at the piano, Father tried to make up for her. Every day he threw candies to me when I stood on the bal-cony to wave goodbye to him on his way to work. He showered me with gifts large and small. When I was four, he asked me what I wanted on Three Kings Day, January 6, when South American children receive their holiday gifts. I told him I wanted a real car—our family had never owned one. Early on Three Kings Day a messenger arrived and asked for Señorita Trenchi. Mother, surprised, pointed to me and said I was the only *Miss* Trenchi in the house. The messenger escorted me downstairs and there was a brand new luxurious Hudson car. He handed me the keys and said, "The Three Kings asked me to give you these." Of course I never really got to drive the car, but for all the years we had it, it was registered in my name.

When I was a little older, Father would call me many times a day from his office just to chat. In the evenings he went to his club, but when he was ready to come home he would call me on my private phone and I would go down to the front door to wait for him. Then we would sit and talk about what we had done that day. Sometimes we even shared a small glass of brandy. It was these hours that made my father so dear to me. Without friends my own age and with a mother whose discipline was apt to be harsh, he provided me with an anchor of friendship.

Father and I were always having accidents and illnesses that took us perilously close to death's door. When I was four, just after he had given me the car, he got sick and began to shrink. I worried that he would just disappear one day. Over a period of months, his weight 61 dropped from nearly 200 pounds to about 100, and the doctors gave up hope for his life. But then after 10 months he began eating again and gradually regained his health. Another time, shortly before Mother and I were to leave for Paris, his intestine ruptured in three places. After a long operation, the doctor came out and told Mother that he could not live through the night. She said, "That's your final word. Now we'll wait for God's." They were amazed at her refusal to believe them, and they were even more amazed when my father began to improve.

From the beginning I had similar scrapes. Before I was three, I fell from the top of a slide and suffered a brain concussion. A second incident that I remember more vividly happened when I was eight. We were vacationing at a seaside hotel and Mother asked me to go back up to our room for something she had forgotten. I was in a hurry and didn't want to wait for the elevator operator, so I got on the car, closed the door and ran it myself. When I got to the sixth floor, I opened the inner door and stepped out onto the narrow ledge between it and the outer door. Before I could open the other door, the inner door slammed shut and the elevator car began to go down. I
backed flat against the outer door and

watched the car disappear. My knees felt weak and I was near panic. I began to scream right off, but it took people ten minutes just to discover where I was and it was 45 minutes before the fire department rescued me.

By the time Mother and I left for France, I had grown so close to my father that I didn't know how I would manage without him. The very first day after we arrived in Paris, I insisted that we go down to the steamship company to make reservations for our return to Argentina in ten months. Then I began to count the days.

When Father came to celebrate my fifteenth birthday, I felt that my life had been put back together. But early the next morning I heard my parents quarreling bitterly. I suppose I was aware that they had been drifting apart for some time. But now I could no longer ignore the fact. I felt torn between my obligations to Mother and my need for my father.

That same week, I was to begin preparing for the final competition between all the pianists in the Conservatory. Everyone was told what the set piece would be thirty days before. Then, with a month's preparation, each pianist played it for the judges. But every time I sat down to start practicing with Germaine 63

Pinault, I would have a headache or crying spell. I was at the end of my rope. The fourteen-hour days of study and practice and the sudden realization that my family was pulling apart had been too much.

ᴿ 9

WHEN the headaches and crying spells continued, Mother made an appointment with a doctor. Both she and Germaine Pinault came with me, and I was there when the doctor told them that I had suffered a severe nervous breakdown and should be given a complete rest for three or four months.

That was the moment I learned how strong Mlle. Pinault's determination really was. She herself had lived under the shadow of doctors' orders all her life and she was not about to submit to such orders gracefully. She flew into a rage at the doctor. She told him I couldn't possibly stop practicing. In fact, there were only 24 days until I had to play in a competition at the Conservatory and I hadn't yet been able to start learning the set piece.

The doctor became angry too, but he was no match for Mlle. Pinault. Finally they arranged a compromise. I was to be given a complete rest for twelve days—half the time until the competition. Then Mlle. Pinault and my mother could reimpose their discipline. I was grateful for the short holiday.

For twelve days I wandered through the streets and parks of Paris, rarely speaking to anyone and avoiding music altogether. Mlle. Pinault then volunteered to come to our apartment to teach me to save me the time of traveling, showing us another side of her iron will.

We lived on the fifth floor of a building without an elevator, and her weak heart was hardly equal to the climb. But she never complained. Mother would meet her every morning on the ground floor with a chair. On each landing, Mlle. Pinault would sit down and get her breath before proceeding.

The set piece for the competition was Chopin's Ballade No. 3. The other contestants had already had more than two weeks to learn it. But now, Mlle. Pinault's teaching methods came to the rescue. Not a moment was lost, and in twelve days I was prepared.

The only uncertainty was my nerves. As the day drew near, I began to worry about breaking down again. And on the day of the contest, waiting outside the hall with Mother and Mlle. Pinault, I burst into tears. Mlle. Pinault simply sent Mother away and encouraged me to cry to relieve my tension. Scarcely had I

finished than it was time to go to the "room

of terror," the small room just offstage where pianists had to wait alone while the person just before them played.

Then it was my turn.

Terrified, I butchered the first page of the Ballade, playing it so badly that I wanted to get up and run away. But then I thought of Mlle. Pinault and all she had gone through in the past weeks. How disappointed she would be if I quit now! That morning I had received a cable from Monsignor Franceschi in Buenos Aires wishing me good fortune. He, too, would be disappointed and so would my father and mother. I took a deep breath and tore into the rest of it. From that moment on my fingers seemed to fly over the keys. And when the results of the competition were announced a few hours later, I had won! Mlle. Pinault's determination had seen me through.

That summer when Mother and I returned to Buenos Aires we discovered that dictator Juan Peron had frozen all my father's assets, bringing his businesses to a complete halt. Although we still lived in our handsome apartment with many beautiful things, we had no money. Shortly after we arrived Mother decided that the only way we could be sure of returning to Paris in October was to sell our car. For ten weeks we advertised it, but no one seemed interested in buying it. The week before we were supposed to leave, she told me to unpack—there was no money for us to fly to Paris. But then, on the last possible day, a man called and wanted to buy the car. Fifteen hours later, Mother and I were on the plane.

We had agreed that I should continue at the Conservatory, which was free as long as I could do well in the entry competition, and that perhaps I could also manage one lesson a week with Yves Nat. But there was simply no way to pay Mlle. Pinault for her five-hour-a-day lessons.

Shortly after our arrival, Germaine Pinault called to say that she heard about our financial difficulties and would be glad to teach me without payment for as long as our problems lasted. Typically, she insisted on the same demanding schedule as before—the situation was never mentioned again.

For the next three years (with time off in the summers) the schedule went on as before. Germaine Pinault took me through vast ranges of piano literature, pushing me all the time to do more, learn faster, play closer to perfection. Such intense exposure to a single artist is something few musicians ever get, and Mlle. Pinault contributed enormously to my development as a performer.

Often her demands seemed superhuman.

Only on rare occasions in all the years I studied with her did she ever compliment me beyond a grudging "Not bad." Though later I learned that she had told Mother again and again how well I was doing. Sometimes we would spend eighteen hours on a single page of music. I would play it over and over until I was crying with frustration and anger. There are a few pieces of music that I still can't stand to play because Mlle. Pinault ruined them for me.

One day in my third year of study with her I got so mad I said, "If I play so badly, why don't I just take my books and go home? I can find something else to do besides playing the piano."

Her immediate reaction was shock at my insubordination. But within seconds she too became angry, shouting at me and accusing me of ignorance as well as ingratitude. At this I picked up my books and fled from her apartment. As I was leaving, she called after me: "And don't ever come back."

At first I was relieved. But on the subway ride home I began to think about the consequences of my action. What would I tell Mother? How could I explain that I had quit my studies with Mlle. Pinault and insulted her? When I got off the subway I found a pay phone and called Mlle. Pinault to apologize and to ask if I could come the next day as usual. She accepted my apology and said of course. Then I went home and told Mother that I was home early because Mlle. Pinault had not been feeling well.

Germaine Pinault was a difficult teacher to work under. But as I grew older I began to see that she just assumed others were as single-minded and determined as she. Her system of teaching was skillfully organized and far-reaching. Yet even more important to me was her insistence on single-mindedness. The way she forced me to practice after my nervous breakdown, though seemingly cruel and senseless, caused me to recognize how strong the human personality can be and how much potential we all have if pushed to develop and use it.

✤ 10

MY FATHER, in Argentina, began to live a life more and more independent of us after his break with Mother that day in Paris. He gave up most of his old friends and none of us knew the people in his new circle. Still he lived at home until shortly after I turned nineteen, when I was studying in Buenos Aires toward an Argentine degree. Then he moved out and it became more difficult for me to see him. We met occasionally at his office or in a coffee house, but I resented not being a part of his new life. We would often quarrel. Sharing the same strong will and hot temper, we knew only too well how to hurt each other.

The final break came in September 1961, just before I left for my concert tour of Europe. He had given me a beautiful ring when I was 19. Then during one of our arguments he made me give it back. Now, I asked him to return it. He refused. I got angry and began to shout all the cruel things I could 71 think of. Finally he put the ring in my hand saying, "I hope your plane crashes and I don't have to see you again."

The memory of that remark stuck in my mind three or four months later when Dr. Rivadeau-Duma asked if my family could pay for my operation. I had refused to call him but my father had saved me anyway. Now I was on a plane about to take off for Buenos Aires and would soon see him for the first time since that argument. I prayed that everything might be different and that Father and I could be friends once again.

The plane trip was a nightmare. The airline would not have allowed me to fly if they had known my condition. When the plane started to ascend, I thought I was going to die. By that time I was pretty experienced in pain, having felt many kinds and many intensities. But whenever the pressure changed in the cabin, I thought my head was going to explode. At the start I was all dressed up; an expensive wig hid the fact that my own hair was hardly an inch long. After an hour, I didn't care how funny I looked. I took the wig off, hoping that it might give me some relief, but it didn't.

The trip from Paris to Buenos Aires was to take 36 hours—with intermediate stops at

Madrid, Dakar, Rio de Janeiro, Sao Paulo, and

Montevideo. When we began our descent into Madrid, I discovered that coming down was worse than going up. Mercifully I fainted, but when I came to I realized that that was just the beginning. Mother did what she could, and the Air France stewards were as helpful as they could be. Then in Rio Mother got off the plane—her ticket called for a transfer—and left me to fly the last part of the trip alone.

I remember that last leg with unnatural clarity. Flying—and especially coming home —had always been an emotional experience for me. Now the combination of emotion and pain made the impression overwhelming. I began to realize that when I arrived my father would be at the foot of the stairs. Other passengers would have to wait to see their families in the terminal; but my father, an important import-export businessman, would be just outside the plane.

As we approached Buenos Aires, I went back to the rest room to put my wig back on and to replace my make-up. I was dizzy and unsteady, but my anticipation was so great that I hardly noticed. Just as I was finishing, the pilot spoke on the intercom. "Ladies and gentlemen," he said first in French then in Spanish, "in thirty minutes we will be arriving in Ezeiza International Airport in the city of Buenos Aires." My heart leapt—it seemed 73

I had been gone half a lifetime and now how wonderful to be back home!

But as the plane began to pressurize, I was suddenly struck by a great wave of dizziness. I still remember fighting so hard to stay conscious as everything whirled around me faster and faster. Then I fell. . . .

The next thing I remember, I was being carried down the steps of the plane in a stretcher. The pilot had called the airport and asked that an ambulance be waiting. I realized where we were and struggled to sit up. My father! I must see my father. The attendant pushed me down gently. "Quiet, miss," he said. "You are very sick." Still I craned my neck to see all the faces staring down at me. Then I saw the familiar face of one of my father's employees, a man I had known for years, and my heart sank. If he was here, my father wasn't.

"You fainted on the plane," he told me. "They're taking you to the hospital for an examination. Then I'll drive you home."

On the way home he tried to explain that my father had been kept away by a business emergency. But I knew that nothing would keep Raul Trenchi from doing anything he really wanted to do. If he hadn't come, he was still angry with me. "So here we are," I thought, "back where we started from. Nothing has changed."

At home my aunt and several cousins welcomed us. We were happy to see each other, but they were shocked by my appearance and after a few minutes I said that I was tired and went to my bedroom. I wanted to be near the telephone because I was sure that any moment my father would be calling me.

As I lay waiting for his call, my eyes wandered around the room. Everywhere I looked I saw gifts from my father. There was an ancient television set, one of the first ever brought into the country—he had given that to me even before there was any television to watch. Beside my bed was a clock radio built into a lamp, which he had sent to the United States for. Most precious of all was a miniature piano, about three feet high that had four octaves and really played. This he had specially ordered from Tokyo when I was the same size as the piano. Every day, in fact, my father gave me something. Never was there a more generous or thoughtful man.

But now the phone didn't ring. After two hours I began to believe that he wasn't going to call. So I finally swallowed my pride, picked up the phone and, without thinking, dialed his number at work. Even though it was eight in the evening, he was there and answered on the second ring.

Instantly his voice became cold and distant. 75

He asked politely how I was and said he was glad I was home; but he was just doing his duty. And that made me very sad.

An hour later Mother arrived after taking her later flight from Rio. We ate a light supper and went straight to bed.

11

DR. RIVADEAU-DUMA had advised me not to play the piano for two or three months until I had recovered my strength. But there was simply no possibility of this. Across the room I could see my piano. It was an English upright, a gift from my father. Having imported it for a client, he had made the mistake of sending me down to the warehouse to try it out. I fell in love with it and begged him to buy it for me even though we had nine or ten others, six of which were grands. Father had to pay the client twice what it was worth to make up for the inconvenience of his having to wait for another piano to be shipped. But for years, the English upright had remained a favorite of mine.

Now I decided just what I would play first —the familiar Mozart Sonata in C. I would get the music out in case my memory failed, but I could already hear myself playing it! Three months had passed since I had fled from the hospital to play in Mme. Roche's apartment— 77 it seemed like an eternity.

Mother helped me over to the piano as I was still very weak and dizzy. I was almost overcome with excitement. I just sat there staring at the keys until Mother said, "Well, are you ready to start?"

"Yes," I replied and raised my hands. But suddenly, when I raised my fingers to strike the first note, a terrible pain shot through my head. Tears came to my eyes and I thought I was going to fall off the stool. I waited a few minutes, then tried again more cautiously. But this time the pain was stronger than ever. I nearly lost consciousness. Somehow Mother got me to bed and brought me a pain killer that Dr. Rivadeau-Duma had prescribed.

"Well, it's just the effects of the long trip and the change in climate and time zones," I told myself. "If I rest a while everything will be all right." But that afternoon when I tried to play again, the pain came as strongly as ever. And the next morning was the same.

That afternoon Mother packed a suitcase full of test results and reports from my Paris doctors and we went to see a neurologist in Buenos Aires. He read what we had brought and asked me all kinds of questions—some so silly that I thought *he* was sick. Then he took an electroencephalogram. I still remember the

crazy patterns my brain waves made on that

machine: squiggles, followed by nothing for several seconds, then more squiggles. The doctor told me that I was still in bad shape and that my recovery would be a difficult one. Dr. Rivadeau-Duma had told me the same thing, but I thought he was exaggerating, the way doctors often do, telling me the worst possible so that nothing would disappoint me.

I returned home and began to work at playing the piano again. First I would have to learn to move my fingers and tolerate the pain. I went to the keyboard. I closed it and put my fingers carefully down on the wooden case. Slowly and laboriously I concentrated on moving them one at a time, lifting them slightly and putting them down again. The pain was intense, but since I didn't have to push hard enough to make a sound, I could control it by how high I lifted each finger and how hard I brought it down. I practiced for ten minutes, then went to bed, exhausted.

Every day I was able to do a little more— but only a very little. And I still ached to play on the keys and make music. Once in awhile when I felt better than usual, I tried a few notes, but this always sent me back to bed, regretting it.

During these early weeks I often fainted without warning. This frightened Mother so much that one day as I recovered consciousness I heard her crying. "Please don't die, please don't die," she said; "if you do, I don't know how I shall keep living." Until that moment I had always had the impression my mother hated me. But now I knew that however harsh she might be she really did care.

After a few weeks, I started to gain strength —although my piano practice was still going slowly and painfully. I could stay up for half a day now, but I was beginning to realize that my memory problems would go beyond memorizing music. Often in the middle of a conversation I would forget the subject and even to whom I was talking. I would forget where I put my keys or left a book. It was incredibly frustrating.

By the time I had been home a month, however, I could at least look at myself in the mirror without becoming disgusted; so I went out more often, saw some old friends and found happiness in simply being alive. It was fall in Argentina, a beautiful time of year.

As my outside interests grew, I began drifting away from the piano where all was still frustration. Dr. Rivadeau-Duma's words kept returning—"Don't play . . . you will only receive bitterness and disappointment for your pains." Perhaps he was right, I told myself. After all, I was still young and attractive. I had friends and money to spend, and my health was improving every day. Maybe I should look for a husband and forget about the piano. Who could blame me?

To celebrate my birthday at the end of May, I decided to have a big party. After inviting all my friends, I went out and bought a dress as well as a stack of new records.

The day came, May 29. Winter was approaching, and the weather was cold for Buenos Aires. That night everyone arrived, and as the evening wore on things couldn't have been happier. I was alive and well.

But sometime after midnight, I suddenly began to feel depressed. Within minutes I broke into tears and was soon nearly hysterical. I still don't know what brought this on, but I do remember that the party came to a sudden halt. I also remember looking down at my hands again and again and crying, "I can't move my fingers! I can't move my fingers!" The guests soon went home and Mother helped me to bed.

The next morning Mother was furious at me for making such a scene. She and Father, who always held their emotions inside, hated public displays. All the next day I lay in bed trying to understand myself and the circumstances I found myself in. I knew that I was crazy to think I could suddenly become just a fun-loving rich girl on the lookout for a husband. My life had been organized for a different purpose. And now, even though every movement of my fingers caused me real pain, playing the piano was still my life. I began to realize that I had been trying to escape.

I also thought that day about God's plan for me. Mother had always believed that God's hand could be seen in what others considered accidents or pure chance. From the time I was small she had taught me that talent is a gift from God and that people with talent must account for it. But why had God saddled me with such misfortune? Why had He made it so painful and difficult for me to play? It seemed cruel and unfair. But the more I thought about it, the more certain I became that the accident was His way of testing me as to whether I really did want to use my talent. Monsignor Franceschi had taught me that God is a personal Being who stands with and helps people who believe in Him. The Monsignor had died when I was 19, and his last words were a blessing to me. I recalled that moment and felt again that God would not let me down if I did not let Him down.

All through that day and part of the night I reviewed my situation. When I woke up the next morning, I felt stronger and more sure of myself than I had for years. I now believed that I knew where I was going. A great burden of uncertainty had been lifted from me. My recovery began that morning. There would be other discouragements and setbacks, and the road would be long, but that day I set my course. I was going to be a pianist.

✑ 12

DURING the first year after the accident I began to understand what part of my condition was temporary and what part was likely to be permanent.

The first thing to be faced was pain. Little by little it began to disappear as I moved my fingers. I suppose the brain was healing; or perhaps I just trained myself to block it out. Anyway, I soon saw that I would be able to play the piano without intolerable pain.

But the headaches continued. When Dr. Rivadeau-Duma prescribed pain pills for me before I left Paris, I asked him how long I would need them. "Probably for the rest of your life," he had said. Gradually I came to see that he was right. For days, sometimes weeks at a time, the pains would stay away. But then, without warning, an attack would come. And they were terrible. I learned that I must never go anywhere without my pills; nothing else gave me the slightest relief. To this day, I am more afraid of forgetting my pills than I am of forgetting keys, money or whatever.

My second problem was coordination. Some days I would have no difficulty. Other days, I would be all thumbs. If I reached for a plate, I would get it by the very edge and drop it on the floor. Or simply walking, I would lose my sense of balance or seemingly "forget" how to put one foot in front of the other. Not long ago I was crossing a busy New York street when the light changed. There I stood in the middle, frightened by the cars and for the moment unable to move one way or the other.

My coordination problems were most severe the first year after my accident, but they have never fully disappeared. Yet little by little, I've learned to cope with them. Unlike the headaches, these episodes come on gradually, so I usually have some warning.

As the pain disappeared, I began to realize that after more than 20 years of training, my fingers no longer "knew" what to do. I had to start out like a beginner, concentrating intently on one finger at a time, going over even a simple passage again and again so my fingers could relearn their jobs. It was slow, frustrating business. My mind knew perfectly well what the fingers should be doing, and the fingers themselves, although weak from their three-month vacation, were not damaged in any way. But somehow the communication between the mind and the fingers had been damaged, so I had to sit down and relearn what I had spent half my life learning once before. At first I could play only a few measures; then my concentration would flag and my fingers would get all mixed up. Slowly I stretched these few measures into one page, then to two pages. But even after I began to play in public again I had to concentrate so hard that I would be drenched with perspiration after playing even the shortest piece.

Luckily, I could fall back on a long tradition of discipline and hard work. First with my mother and then with Germaine Pinault in Paris, I had been drilled on piano technique to within an inch of my life. I know hundreds of exercises by heart, and had been thoroughly taught the mechanics of playing. Putting all this together, I organized a program of practice that would slowly but surely bring back my strength and technique. Within six months I could sit at the piano for three or four hours, and I began to be encouraged by my progress.

As my technique returned, I began to test my memory, and was upset to discover that my "ear memory" was completely gone. I had once been able to hear a simple piece, then go

to the piano and play it note for note. Now

even with familiar music, my ear could not tell my fingers what came next.

Most of the pieces I had played before the accident came back to me, especially those I had played for many years. But even so, there were odd gaps—passages that I could not remember no matter how hard I tried. New material I could play with the music in front of me. But once the music was out of sight I couldn't remember a single note—often not even the first measure. The doctors had warned me about this strange memory disability, and of course I already knew that I was forgetful in everyday matters. Still, it was hard to accept that I would never be able to learn a new piece and play it without the music flopping around in front of me.

Here again, I fell back on my earlier training. Germaine Pinault had made a special point of teaching me to read music and learn it before ever going to the piano. Once she had given me the whole "Emperor" Concerto by Beethoven. I had 24 hours to learn it without touching the piano. The next day I played the whole thing for her up to tempo and without the music. Of course in those days I had both visual and ear memory to rely on, but the practice of memorizing from the actual page was to prove a great advantage to me now. I picked a few short pieces and began trying to memorize them. After spending two days on the first I thought I had mastered it. But when I sat at the piano on the third morning, every single note had disappeared into a deep dark hole. Only very gradually did I learn how to "fix" a piece in my mind so that it would be there a day or a week later.

That fall, I was beginning to feel like a pianist again, handicapped with a frayed memory and flawed coordination to be sure, but no longer having to apologize for my music. I could now play without spending every ounce of concentration on making a certain finger move or praying that the next phrase would come to mind in time. Yet would I be able to stand the pressure of a public performance?

By April 1963, a year after my return to Buenos Aires, I was restless. Operating all the time under Mother's watchful eye was difficult after my years of independence. Of course it was comforting to be where people could take care of me, but the better I felt the less I enjoyed this interference.

All mothers are much the same, I suppose, treating their children as children long after they have grown into adults. But mine, who had never let me go down to the corner by myself as a child, still felt I needed that kind of supervision. She worried when I went out with friends and scolded me if I didn't return early. Though I tried to understand, I also got angry. She and I began to quarrel the way we had when I was a teenager, only now it was worse.

The breach with my father had never really healed, either. I saw him once in a while, usually in a coffee house or at his office. He was polite but distant. No more showers of gifts and kisses. I was bewildered and resentful of his behavior, but there seemed nothing I could do to change him.

One day in late April I was called by a radio station in La Plata, a city about forty miles from Buenos Aires. The station had just received word that a musician scheduled to appear on a live program late in May was canceling. Would I like to replace him? Right away I thought, "This is the chance I've been waiting for." I said yes. After we had settled on the date and the time, the station manager asked what I would like to play. I thought a moment and then replied that I would play Schumann's *Kreisleriana,* a piece I had always wanted to learn.

The next four weeks I practiced harder than I ever had in my life. Every day I spent eight hours at the piano and another two or three "reading" the score. Although I planned to play with the music, I also wanted to memorize it just to see if I could. Soon my fingers 89 were raw and my back ached constantly. But when the time came I had learned the piece well.

Mother drove me to La Plata on the day of the performance. I went to the studio to warm up on the piano. It was a nice little hall to play in, and I felt good. I planned to take two pain pills just before the concert to make sure no headache would strike during my playing. My coordination was good; and since I would have the music in front of me, even though I had learned the piece by memory, everything was under control.

Mother and I went out for a bite to eat. I was amazed at how calm and confident I felt. When we returned to the studio, we talked to the announcer and learned exactly how the program would go. As air time approached, a few people came in to the hall and sat down and my mother joined them as I took my place at the piano.

I heard the announcer introducing me over the loudspeaker (he was in another studio). Then all of a sudden I heard someone else. Dr. Rivadeau-Duma seemed to be right in front of me, and he was saying, "Don't try to play in public. Your mind will not work under pressure. Don't . . . don't . . . don't . . ."

For a moment I was paralyzed with fear.
But then, as would happen so often, this fear

turned to anger. I was angry at the doctor and at myself for being so scared. Just as the announcer was saying "And now, Ana Maria Trenchi," I grabbed the music off the piano and flung it out into the audience where I would have no chance to retrieve it. *There,* I thought, now let me play this well *and* by memory.

Looking back, I'm a little amazed at myself. But I did play well. And when it was over I carried on like a child, I was so excited. That night Mother and I celebrated. It was only an insignificant radio performance, but it seemed a huge step forward.

When I sat down the next morning to work out a few spots in the *Kreisleriana* that needed some improvement, I discovered to my horror that I could not remember one note of the piece. I closed my eyes to concentrate and tried all kinds of little memory tricks, but nothing worked. In fact, it would be years before I could play that piece from memory again.

13

BY AUGUST 1963 my situation in Buenos Aires was becoming less and less happy. Mother and I were at odds, I rarely saw my father and I had nothing very interesting to do musically. After La Plata I received no other invitations to play and felt shut out of Argentina's musical life.

Music in Buenos Aires had always been a rather closed and exclusive circle. On returning from Paris five years earlier, I had discovered this. Even Mother with her music school was considered outside the small circle of people who controlled music in Buenos Aires. After Paris I had taken advanced degrees at the Conservatory and university in Buenos Aires, completing a six-year course at the latter in less than two years and had studied with Alberto Ginastera, the most prominent living Argentine composer. Under Mother's guidance I had also won a number of important South American competitions. But even these accomplishments did not enable me to pursue a career as a soloist. Because of my training in Paris and my lack of proper connections in Argentina, I was a foreigner in my own country.

Once I even played a trick on the musical establishment to show how partial they could be. A scholarship for advanced study in Vienna had been offered, and I submitted an application. One requirement was that applicants send tape recordings of their performances. Knowing I had no chance to win, I put together a tape featuring Artur Schnabel, Walter Gieseking, Vladimir Horowitz, and Arthur Rubinstein, four of the great pianists in the world. A few weeks later I received a letter from the committee explaining that I didn't have the promise required for the scholarship. I wonder what they were after.

My lack of a future in Argentina now began to depress me and I felt that I had to get away for a while. I asked Mother if she would help me pay for a vacation in Europe. She agreed, and I made plans to leave late in August.

Although I have traveled a great deal in my life, trips remain a very emotional experience for me. I remember that departure from Buenos Aires particularly. On the one hand, I was excited and looking forward to the relaxation and freedom I would have away from home. But I also remembered how sick I had 93 been in the past months and how much care I had needed. Would I be able to cope with my headaches outside the family? Would my occasional clumsiness and lapses of memory give me trouble? I began to doubt whether I was ready for all this. As I said goodby to Mother, I felt like crying. She understood my feelings and encouraged me. "You will be fine," she said. "Don't be afraid. God will be with you." All at once I was just another traveler on my way to a vacation.

Geneva is one of my favorite cities. And since a musical competition was about to begin there, it was filled with young musicians, some of whom were friends from my Paris days. We spent long hours at coffee houses and in bars talking music and enjoying ourselves. How different this was from my life at home in Argentina. Although I was 24 years old, I had never spent much time with people my own age, and now I discovered how much fun it could be. From Switzerland I went to France.

Paris in the early fall is particularly beautiful. I wandered around the city, went to concerts, and spent endless hours gossiping about unimportant things with old friends. One day I passed the church of La Madeleine. Of course I remembered the last time I had been there on that cold winter night after the accident. Now, lit brilliantly by the sun and surrounded by blue sky, it appeared as a symbol to me of my recovery and my hopes for a new life.

Yet Paris contained a few disappointments as well. The greatest was in my not being able to reach Germaine Pinault. I wanted her to know how much her teaching had helped me recover my skills at the piano after the accident. But she was gone and no one could tell me where.

A second, bitter disappointment was that there seemed no place for me in Paris musically. I had been hoping that I would be offered a chance to play or at least to teach somewhere. After all, so many of my friends were musicians. And they would know what was going on—who, perhaps, was looking for a pianist for a recital or a tour. But no one ever mentioned a single opportunity. Were they worried about my condition, afraid to suggest something beyond my capabilities? I sensed sometimes that they were watching me for signs of weakness or disability, and I was disappointed that they had so little faith in me.

My vacation was coming to an end. There was no reason to stay in Paris any longer, so I went sadly to Swissair and booked a flight home. I knew the situation was no better there, but I didn't have much choice. After writing Mother, to warn her of my arrival, I began to say my farewells. The trip had become simply a happy interlude between two long stays in Argentina.

But on Wednesday, October 14, I got a call that changed the direction of my life.

14

WHEN I answered the telephone at my hotel that morning, I was surprised by the voice of Nadia Boulanger. Mlle. Boulanger, who had taught many of the major composers, conductors and performers of the last forty years, was then in her seventies and one of the most famous personalities in the musical world. I also had studied with her, attending some of her master classes while I was a student in Paris. And when I was in the hospital just before the operation she had sent me a note offering her prayers for a speedy recovery. But I had not seen her during my visit. What could she be calling about?

Through the French Ministry of Cultural Affairs she had just received an urgent request from Kunitachi University in Tokyo for a French-trained teacher of piano. Would I be interested?

I didn't know what to say. Of course I was looking for just such an opportunity. But Japan? Stalling for time, I asked her how soon 97 the new teacher was needed. She said that the Conservatory wanted the person to start teaching on Tuesday—only six days away—and had sent air fare. I explained that I had been planning to return home to Buenos Aires in a few days and that I would need at least a few minutes to make up my mind. Could I call her back in half an hour? She agreed.

Then I sat down to think. I felt dazed and unsure. Never had I made such a big decision all by myself. What did I know about Tokyo or the University there? Nothing. The appointment was for two years. If I decided to go and it turned out to be a mistake, I would suffer the consequences for a long time. Still, what choices did I have? I wasn't ready to become a full-time performer again. Nor was there anything for me in Paris or Buenos Aires. On the other hand, I needed to be involved in music and I had done some teaching. Mother and Germaine Pinault had often told me that I would be a good teacher, although I had trained to be a performer. And Tokyo appealed to my sense of adventure.

My head was still spinning when I called Mlle. Boulanger to accept the appointment.

The next few days were a blur of activity and strong emotions. I composed a long telegram to Mother, describing the offer and asking her opinion, then waited nervously for the reply. "Go," it said.

The next day a friend I had met in Geneva arrived in Paris. I told him that I had decided to go to Tokyo and he thought I was joking. When I finally persuaded him I was serious, however, he told me that my decision was a foolish one and tried to persuade me to change my mind. On Saturday evening, my last in Paris, we danced until two in the morning. Five hours later, I was on a plane to Japan.

I slept until we landed in Geneva. But when the plane took off again, the man sitting next to me asked in bad French where I was going. I told him that I was an Argentine pianist going to Tokyo and his eyes lit up. It turned out he was a Uruguayan diplomat on his way to India. He was so happy to find someone who spoke Spanish that he asked me to have a Scotch with him to celebrate our meeting. I protested that it was much too early (10 in the morning) and that I didn't really feel like a drink (after nearly 48 hours without sleep), but without effect.

The man behind the plane's small bar noticed immediately that we were speaking Spanish, and he began to speak it, too. Although Swiss, he had lived for some years in Mexico. Thus began an eighteen-hour party.

Our bartender provided food and as much Scotch as we could drink, and soon he joined us. We chattered, told jokes, and even sang songs for a while. By the time we reached Bombay, where both men were to end their journeys, we had gone through three bottles of Scotch and were working on the fourth. How I managed to stay awake all this time, I shall never know. But it was a wonderful party. Before they got off, we exchanged addresses and swore we'd write to each other. But of course we never did.

Finally I got some sleep as the plane flew across Asia. I awoke shortly before we landed at Hong Kong, which must be one of the world's most beautiful cities with its steep hills and the bay filled with sampans and fishing boats. It was incredible to see whole neighborhoods of shacks only a few blocks from skyscrapers and modern mansions atop nearby hills. I knew I would love this city and promised to return.

Nearly all the passengers got off the plane in Hong Kong, and soon we were aloft again. It was a rough flight through a storm, but finally the pilot spoke over the intercom: "Ladies and gentlemen," he said, "in thirty minutes we will be landing at Tokyo International Airport."

Suddenly it hit me. Tokyo? What was I

doing here? How had I ever decided to come to this far corner of the world? It was as if I was waking from a long sleep. My apprehensiveness did not lessen when I walked into the strange airport. Everyone was speaking either Japanese or English and I understood neither. On top of this, the man who was to meet me at the immigration desk with papers allowing me to enter the country was not there; and I couldn't explain my situation to the officials. I remembered my friend in Paris who had begged me not to come and said out loud, "Why didn't I listen to you?"

ᕲ 15

AT 11:30 P.M., an hour and a half after we landed, the man with my entry papers finally arrived. He was a Frenchman who taught in Tokyo and I had known him briefly in Paris. Though he was upset for being late, I was furious and unleashed my Latin temper. Instantly I was sorry. My nerves were on edge from the long trip, sleeplessness and alcohol. He understood this; and as soon as I apologized, we were friends again.

He took me to a hotel where most of the Western teachers stayed, a beautiful American-style place across from the Imperial Palace. When the bellboy showed me my room all I wanted to do was fall across its elegant queen-sized bed and go to sleep. But the Frenchman, still upset about being so late to pick me up, invited me to have a drink with him; and because I wanted to make up for my bad manners, I accepted his invitation.

Shortly thereafter I went to my room. It was 3 A.M., and my first workday was to begin at nine. I would be meeting the director of the University, its staff, my translators and some of my students. Surprisingly, when I woke up and took a shower I felt almost as good as new. At breakfast in the hotel dining room I met a number of the other Western teachers. They were so friendly that I began to relax and feel that my stay here might actually be fun. One surprise at breakfast was the background music—Tchaikovsky's Violin Concerto.

The people I would be working with included three young Japanese girls who would be my interpreters. They spoke French well, and I was relieved to find that we could understand each other. I was also impressed by my students. Some were superb pianists already and all of them seemed eager to learn.

Still, the first lessons proved difficult. Half the time seemed taken up with translations, and I never quite understood the delays.

I would say to the interpreter, "Can he play something else?"

The interpreter would turn and talk to the student for two minutes, and the student would then take two minutes to reply. The interpreter would then say to me, "He's not sure he understands your question."

This drove me crazy. So I learned to think carefully before I said anything. Often I would just demonstrate something on the piano, which the students were quick to pick up. It was incredible how my Japanese students could hear a passage played and then play it exactly the same way. They were like tape recorders.

I was scheduled to teach at the University three days a week, which gave me a fair amount of time for my own practice. But first I had to find a piano. I asked the management of the hotel if I could move a rented one into my room. They said they would have to think about it. I waited ten days, then asked again. Well, they said, maybe—we'll have to wait and see. I didn't know what to make of this indecision. Then one day after I had been waiting more than a month, I happened to mention the situation at the Argentine consulate. Everyone began to laugh. The Japanese, it was explained to me, are very reluctant to say "no" because they think it's impolite. If they tell you "maybe" they almost always mean "no."

Several kind people offered me their pianos for practice. One woman who had a Yamaha upright in her house was only a block from the hotel. She let me know I could come any time to practice, and I was most grateful. But there was a catch. After I had been practicing

for an hour or so she would come in and offer

me tea or something to eat. We would then sit down on tatami mats to drink tea and she would begin to talk—in Japanese—even though she must have known I didn't understand a word. At first I tried to think of other things, but she was very sensitive and knew right away when I wasn't listening.

Eventually I got fairly good at "understanding" her. I could tell right away what kind of mood she was in and I could follow her changing emotions as she spoke. Still, I came to dread these "conversations." I began coming to her house at odd times, hoping to miss her. But this was impossible. Morning or evening, weekday or weekend, she would always appear to offer her hospitality. Yet even with these delays, I managed to spend many hours at her piano learning all the sonatas of Mozart and Beethoven. For busy as I was, I was determined to become a performer once again.

The most frequently heard piece of music during my stay in Tokyo was the Tchaikovsky Violin Concerto. At breakfast the second morning, I was surprised that it was playing again. It was playing on the third morning, too, and the fourth and the fifth. For a while I expected that some day I would come down and hear something else, but I never did. In the following months I must have heard the concerto more than three hundred times, always with breakfast. The concerto, it turned out, was the maître d's favorite music and he would allow nothing else to be played. Today when I hear the piece, I suddenly taste fried eggs and orange juice and remember every detail of that hotel dining room.

There were lots of things to get used to in Tokyo. And sometimes during those early months I felt I couldn't bear the place another minute. On three occasions I packed my bags and was ready to leave, but each time friends dissuaded me. They said that if I would only stay for a few more weeks I would come to love the Japanese. Eventually I did, but it took a while.

Several times members of the staff were invited to the home of a prominent woman for tea, and we were told that it would be impolite to refuse. I'll never forget the first tea I attended. Before going, I was worried that no one else would speak French, but I soon found that didn't matter. Ushered into a room where twelve or fifteen Japanese ladies were sitting on mats, I sat down clumsily and was handed a cup of tea. Then I waited for someone to start talking. But no one ever did. For the next hour we all sat quiet as mice. If someone caught the eye of someone else, each would smile, take a small sip from her cup and give 106 a little nod. That was it.

The Japanese attitude toward marriage disturbed me. I had been brought up in a house where husband and wife were both strong people (even when they disagreed). And if they didn't get along, they had only themselves to blame since they courted for nearly five years before marrying. In Japan a woman sometimes doesn't even meet the man who is to be her husband until the day of their wedding. And when I saw wedding parties I used to feel so sorry for the bride, who usually sat off by herself with her eyes cast down.

Often I got the impression in homes I visited that the man had absolute control. One night a group of us were having dinner at the home of an important businessman. Toward the end of the meal somebody asked him where his wife was. "Oh, she is eating in the kitchen," he said.

Another puzzlement was the way the Japanese considered time. I once was to meet a Japanese friend at two in the afternoon and she arrived at ten in the morning. When I suggested that perhaps she was a little early she said, "In all of eternity, what difference can a few hours make?" At the same time the Japanese can be the most precise people, as when the Emperor is to attend a public function. Then the schedule of events appears in the newspaper worked out to the very *minute*. 107

For all these new experiences, my teaching was soon going very well—better in fact than I had any reason to hope. I was invited to give three master classes in the auditorium in front of all the students and faculty. I sat at the piano on stage and talked very loudly in French about a certain piece of music while the fastest of my three interpreters translated for the audience. The classes were so successful that I was asked to give three more in a big hall in downtown Tokyo. Soon I was flooded with requests for private lessons. A lovely woman who had lived in Paris and whose daughter had studied piano in Vienna offered to let me teach on her beautiful Steinway grand. Soon I was working with individual students three days a week, many of whom were music teachers at the University.

When I began teaching privately, I found one Japanese custom most touching. No student ever handed me money for the lesson. Instead, each brought a small gift wrapped in colorful paper. Inside, along with the gift was the money. Every night I went back to my hotel loaded down with little packages. It seemed an elegant way to do business.

Often I thought of Germaine Pinault who had taught me in Paris. I differed from most piano teachers in that I concentrated on show-

ing my students *how to learn* and *how to practice*.

Others usually helped their students perfect a particular phrase or movement—they coached them, but they didn't actually teach them much. Now I began to realize that my approach was the one I had learned from Mlle. Pinault. I had never fully appreciated how much she had taught me. Nor had I ever really thanked her for all she had done.

This began to prey on my mind. So one day I placed a call to her in Paris. When I finally got through, her telephone rang and rang. I asked the operator to check the Paris hospitals —Mlle. Pinault had never been well and in recent years she had spent more and more time in hospitals. I said that it was very important I reach her. The operator agreed to try.

The next morning at 10 o'clock the phone rang. I knew it was my call from Paris, and I jumped to answer it. I had rehearsed all the things I would say just as soon as I heard Mlle. Pinault's voice. The operator was on the line. But instead of connecting me, she said, "I am sorry, Miss Trenchi, but Germaine Pinault died three days ago."

Never in my life had I felt so empty and useless. I reproached myself for not calling her sooner, for not taking more pains to trace her when I was in Paris. It is a sad thing when you put off thanking someone until it is too late.

Years later I would help establish the Germaine Pinault International Musical Society, a nonprofit organization devoted to aiding young musicians. I hope that the work of the society will be at least a small tribute to this great but little-known woman.

✣ 16

GERMAINE PINAULT would have been proud of me during my stay in Japan. Not only was I teaching, but I was beginning to perform again. After a successful recital in Tokyo, I went on to play in India, Bangkok, and Hong Kong.

These recitals were a perfect way for me to get back in the habit of performing. For one thing, I had resolved *not* to test my memory just then and always played with the music lying flat in front of me in case I needed it. Also, I stuck with music that I had known for years, and this too gave me a sense of confidence. Finally, since I was playing for audiences I didn't know, I needn't concern myself with what so-and-so would think or whether so-and-so was there.

Japanese audiences love music and are very discriminating. But they don't applaud wildly like a Paris or Buenos Aires audience. In fact, they are incredibly restrained, which came as a bit of a shock the first time I performed.

Wherever I played I met my countrymen because the nearest Argentine embassy or consulate would usually sponsor a reception in my honor after the performance. This is a lovely custom and I would enjoy the company of young diplomatic officers far into the night. I remember these occasions with great fondness as there was much laughter and fun.

One evening, after only a few weeks in Tokyo, I was talking to a handsome young attache at just such a party when a waiter came around offering *sake,* the plum brandy so popular among the Japanese. My companion warned me to drink the small cup of *sake* slowly. Just to tease him, I drank it down in one gulp and called for more. Shortly after my third I suddenly felt as if a hammer had hit me on the back of the head. I knew in a moment that I was very drunk and might pass out at any moment. "Please get me out of here," I begged. Gallantly he made an excuse for us and took me back to my hotel in his car. The next morning I woke up with a terrible headache and a determination not to drink *sake* ever again.

I was able to visit the beautiful city of Hong Kong several times during my stay in Tokyo, but each trip was accompanied by a small disaster. My first arrival set the pattern. After playing a recital in Bangkok, I arrived in Hong

Kong on a Lufthansa plane. The customs officer asked for a certificate showing that I had been inoculated for cholera but I didn't have one. It seems there was an epidemic of cholera in Bangkok just then, so I was told that I would not be able to enter Hong Kong until I had been inoculated and spent five days in quarantine.

Lufthansa was responsible for the oversight since they were supposed to check on such things before the flight began. I was furious because I was supposed to play a concert in Hong Kong that night. But the officials told me I had no choice except to have the shot immediately and then to fly back and forth between the Orient and Germany for the five-day quarantine period. Not only would Hong Kong not admit me just now, neither would any other country in the world. So that's what I did. I made three round-trip flights to Germany in five days, and I was never so happy to get off a plane in my life.

A prominent doctor in Hong Kong, and a great admirer of musicians, invited me to practice on his beautiful Steinway piano before my recitals in his large house overlooking the harbor. One afternoon I was playing for a friend at the doctor's house when he appeared with a gleam in his eye to say that he had a real treat for us. A few minutes later out came an enormous tray of Russian caviar. "This is for you," he said proudly.

I nearly died. Of all the things I can't stand, it's caviar. Even to look at it makes me weak in the legs. And my friend felt the same way. We were both terribly embarrassed but we had to decline. Our beaming Chinese host soon stopped beaming.

The reviews of my recitals in Hong Kong were all good with one exception. The headline in an English-language newspaper read: MISS TRENCHI PLAYS HORRIBLE RECITAL. I knew little English, but the word "horrible" was one word I did understand. This reviewer went on to say that I should close my piano and spend the rest of my days cooking and cleaning house. My friend, who had read this to me, laughed and said that this particular critic disliked women and seldom wrote anything favorable about them. That relieved me somewhat, but I still concluded that my recital had been less than perfect.

Toward the end of June, classes at the University ended for the summer. I kept a few private students, but I still had a lot of extra time. Often I went to Yamaha, a big music store in Tokyo, to practice in one of their small studios. And I spent a great deal of time in Takashimaya, an enormous department

store, just wandering around looking at everything from kitchen pans to fur coats.

The weather got very hot—a different kind of heat than I had ever experienced—but I was determined to enjoy it. All through July I taught a little, practiced a little and amused myself.

One particularly hot night in early August I went for a walk along the moat that separated the hotel from the Imperial Palace and for some reason I began thinking about my dog, a beautiful German Shepherd who had slept at the foot of my bed all the time I was recovering from the accident. Before I knew it I was starting to discover reasons why I should go back to Argentina for the rest of the holidays. After all, I had eight weeks left. I could visit the United States on the way and perhaps line up an appointment to go there after my second year in Tokyo. I had always wanted to live in the United States. Yes, and I knew people in Los Angeles and New York. And I could see my mother and father. . . .

I decided not to make any final plans that night because in the morning it might all seem a silly dream. But when morning came, I was even more ready to go. One of the first telegrams I sent was to a family in St. Louis that I had met earlier in the year in Tokyo. They had suggested that if I ever wanted to study or teach in America, perhaps Washington 115

University in St. Louis would be interested. Back came a letter of welcome; they would arrange interviews and an audition with professors in the music department. So I organized my trip around St. Louis with short stops in Hawaii, San Francisco and Los Angeles. I would fly home from New York.

As the day for my departure drew near, I began to have second thoughts; Tokyo had never seemed a friendlier place. I was given a lovely farewell dinner and both my translators and students appeared at the airport to present me a beautiful pearl ring. With tears in my eyes I waved goodbye, fully expecting to be back in eight weeks.

The university in St. Louis seemed like a dream come true. All the schools I had attended were in the middle of large cities, housed in nondescript buildings. Expecting this, I was swept away by the American campus with its traditional and modern buildings, grass and trees. It all seemed straight from a movie. I played for members of the music department and was told that an assistantship could probably be arranged for a year from September when my appointment was over in Tokyo. I would teach piano and take courses for an American degree. This excited me. For 116 years I had dreamed of living in the United

States. Now at last my future was beginning to take shape.

Soon I was on my way home once more, having completed my first junket around the world in a little less than a year. As usual, when the plane touched down on Argentine soil I cried. Mother had been so impatient to see me that she hadn't called to find out whether my plane was on time; she had been waiting nearly six hours, waving at every incoming plane.

✁ 17

MOTHER and I had so many things to talk about after our year apart. And a few days later Father and I had a long lunch together. He was tremendously interested in Japan and promised to visit me when I returned. We had not had such a happy meeting for years.

That same afternoon I was to meet my mother at her attorney's office, and this led to a different kind of excitement than lawyers' offices usually offer. Adolfo Bottazzi was a handsome man six years older than I; he was both a talented pianist and a very good lawyer. Since I was a teenager I had been told, "He is the right man for you." Now I found him to be as handsome and interesting as others had suggested. We talked so much about my life abroad and about music that Mother never got a chance to bring up her business. When Adolfo invited me to a concert, I accepted happily.

118   During the next few weeks we saw each

other almost every day. Then one evening I had tickets to a concert at the University's School of Law auditorium. Adolfo was to go with me, but while I was dressing the phone rang. The caller introduced himself as Bruno Bottazzi, Adolfo's younger brother. Bruno said that one of his brother's clients had been put in jail and that Adolfo had already left to attend to the matter. So he wouldn't be able to go to the concert with me. I was disappointed, but I thanked Bruno for calling and hung up.

Then I began to think. I had the tickets anyway. Maybe Bruno would like to come with me. I called him back and he said he would love to go. We made plans to meet under the big clock in the Retiro, the central railroad station near the concert hall, and described what we'd be wearing.

I got there early and went to the ladies' room to check my make-up. After all, I wanted Bruno to bring back a good report of me to his brother. When I returned I saw a man across the waiting room with his back to me. I knew at once that it must be Bruno because even from behind he looked so much like Adolfo. Just as I came up to him he turned around and said, "Ana Maria?" "Bruno?" I replied, and together we laughed at our arranged meeting.

119

That night's concert featured the first performance of the Fifth Piano Concerto by Roberto Garcia Morillo, a prominent Argentinian composer. After intermission the orchestra played "Symphonie Fantastique" by Berlioz, and when it came to the waltz movement I was so overwhelmed by old memories that I began to cry.

Years before, Germaine Pinault had played a complex chord on the piano and asked me to name all the notes. I missed two of them and she had said, "Well, you don't have perfect pitch as I had thought. Otherwise you would never have missed that."

Later the same week Mlle. Pinault had gone with Mother and me to a performance of "Symphonie Fantastique." Just as the waltz began, I thought of a way to make her think better of my ear. Hastily I drew two staffs in the margin of the program and wrote out the movement as I heard it. All the way through I was scribbling as fast as my hand would go (the repeats gave me an extra few seconds). When the movement was over, I handed my program to Mlle. Pinault. *"Eh bien!"* she said. It was one of the only compliments she ever made to me.

"What's wrong?" Bruno asked, leaning over. I promised to tell him when the concert was over.

Later we went to a coffee house and talked for nearly three hours. After I told Bruno all about Mlle. Pinault and what she had meant to me, I learned that he too had decided to make his living from music. We had a lovely evening and I went home thinking that Bruno would say nice things about me to his brother.

When I talked to Adolfo the next day, he said, "What have you done to my brother? He can't stop talking about you." I was flattered, but didn't take him seriously. Then a week later Adolfo said to me, "My brother has fallen in love with you. Why don't you go out with him until he gets over it?"

Soon Bruno and I were seeing each other every day. We went for walks, we went to lunch or dinner, we went to concerts. And when we got home we would talk on the telephone until two or three in the morning. In no time I had forgotten all about Adolfo.

But there was one big problem. I was due to fly back to Tokyo in a few weeks. Whenever I thought of leaving, I got a funny feeling—it wasn't Mother or Father or my dog I dreaded leaving, it was Bruno. Still, I made reservations to leave on a Saturday in early October.

The Monday before my flight, Bruno asked me to give up Tokyo and stay in Buenos Aires. He didn't ask me to marry him, just to stay. All that week I was in a turmoil. Should I give up everything in Tokyo and perhaps my future in music for a six-week romance? If I stayed it might all come to nothing and I would be trapped in Argentina once again.

Thursday night Bruno told me he loved me and once more said how much he wanted me to stay. That instant I made up my mind.

The following day I sent a telegram to the director of the university in Tokyo saying that for reasons of health I was unable to return. Within twenty-four hours he answered, saying he was extremely disappointed. I felt terrible at leaving him without a teacher at the last moment, but I was in love.

Bruno and I were inseparable through the Argentinian summer. Late in the season (February), Bruno's family left for Mar del Plata, a fashionable seaside resort where they owned property. They wanted him to go with them as he had always done in the past, but Bruno was determined to stay in Buenos Aires near me. One day Adolfo returned to the city on business. He and Bruno got into a terrible fight. As soon as it was over, Bruno called me and said, "It's getting so bad at home that I think I'm going to have to move out."

"If you're going to move out, why don't we get married?" I asked. The moment it was out I could have bit my tongue off. I had been brought up in a tradition where the woman *never* asks the man to marry her, and here I had done so. There was a silence.

"Would you really marry me?" a voice said.

My mind raced. I hadn't actually thought this through. Did I want to get married? What about my career? Was this some kind of trap I had gotten myself into? But I had asked him, and I couldn't very well back down now. Besides, I really did want to marry him.

"Sure," I said. "Why don't we set a date?"

So right there and then we settled on July 22, five months away. Later we moved the date to August.

For the next week I felt as if I were living in a dream. One minute I was giddy and happy, the next frightened and unsure. The idea of getting married, when it came so close, took some getting used to. And I knew there were two things I had to settle with Bruno before we were officially engaged. The first had to do with my playing the piano.

Already he had become my most severe critic. Every compliment of his was followed by a big "but." I practiced extra hard during those months because I wanted to please him as a musician. Still, Bruno had been born in Italy. His father was Italian, and Bruno had lived there until he was seven. Would he have an "Italian" attitude toward women and marriage? Because if he expected me to give up my performing and become a housewife, I could not marry him. One day I told him how I felt. I was so happy to hear him say that he expected me to go on being a pianist and that he even hoped he could help me get ahead as a performer while he followed his own career as a conductor and teacher. Through good times and bad, he has always kept his word.

The second matter was almost as sensitive. Ever since my first visit to the United States I had been determined to live there one day and I most certainly did not want to spend the rest of my life in Argentina. Bruno knew I had my eye set on St. Louis, but we had not spoken of it since we began to talk about marriage. Most of the people we knew in Argentina resented and disliked the United States. Yes, it was a rich nation, but it was also thought to be un-cultured, ill-mannered, and self-righteous. And the American tourists we saw in Buenos Aires did little to alter this image. Now I real-ized I didn't really know how Bruno felt about America. Perhaps he hated the country as much as most of our acquaintances.

One day I mentioned my wish to live in the United States. He seemed to welcome the idea and even to share my enthusiasm for it. I was so happy! With these things settled I felt more secure about our marriage. From that day on 124 we made plans not only to get married but to move to America soon after. I wrote Washington University to ask about an assistantship for Bruno, who had just graduated from the university in Buenos Aires, and we went to the American embassy to inquire about visas and immigration procedures. There were a hundred things to do, a thousand forms to fill out—and two very upset families to console.

ᘓ 18

WHEN Bruno's mother heard that we were planning to move to America, she was shocked and did not approve. My mother had mixed feelings about our marriage, but her behavior changed with her mood. She seemed to like Bruno well enough, but she also saw her many dreams for me going up in smoke. She knew the problems of combining a family and a career, and she would also be losing her closest companion. Despite our quarrels, we had spent a great deal of time together over the years—at the piano, at home in Buenos Aires, and abroad. And, like Bruno's mother, she was clearly unhappy that we planned to go so far away. Now I can understand her feelings. But at the time, I just wanted her to be happy for me and keep her thoughts to herself.

Bruno's father was ill, and we didn't see much of him. He had been a writer of note, who had pursued his career in both Italy and 126 Argentina. My father was very happy when he learned that I was getting married to Bruno and especially so when I asked him to give me away at the wedding.

Immediately after I asked him I realized that because of the bad feeling between my parents, it would be better if someone else gave me away. Because if he came I was sure my mother would not. Being forced to choose between the two, I felt it had to be Mother.

Though I soon found someone to stand in his place, I failed in one big way. I could not find the courage to tell him what I had done. I don't know whether my father found out through the family or from the newspapers, but it was not until long after the wedding that he would speak to me again. If I called his office, he was "out." Once I even went to his club to ask his forgiveness. But I was only able to leave a note. Not telling Father in person about my change of plans was one of the most thoughtless things I've ever done in my life.

Washington University finally wrote and said that an assistantship for Bruno would be possible, so we began to make plans to fly there in mid-September and moved our wedding to August.

In Argentina there must be a civil ceremony first, then, if the couple wants, a religious ceremony. Most couples have the two weddings within 24 hours. But because we wanted to get passports in our married names and to complete all the immigration details as husband and wife, we scheduled the civil ceremony for August 9 and our church wedding for August 26.

August 9 was sunny but cold. We arrived at the courthouse at noon—Bruno and I and six witnesses, three apiece. My principal witness was Roberto Garcia Morillo, the composer whose music we had heard the night we met. Adolfo stood up for Bruno. The civil ceremony was short but serious and I remember feeling scared and solemn. Then we all went to the Bottazzi's for an elegant four-course lunch with a different wine accompanying each course, of which Bruno and I drank quite a lot. Late that afternoon we went to have our passport photos taken. The next day when we went to pick up our pictures we had difficulty even finding the studio. And when we saw the pictures we knew why. Customs officials— and immigration authorities in the United States—would see us the way we had been that afternoon. Drunk!

Two and a half weeks later the real wedding came, at eight in the evening on Thursday, August 26, in Our Lady of Mercy Cathedral in the heart of Buenos Aires. The date was just one day short of a year since Bruno and I met under the clock at the railroad station.

All day long our house had been in turmoil getting ready for the reception after the wedding, to which 500 people had been invited. Mother was now dressing and my cousin, who was to give me away, was putting on his handsome army uniform. While I was waiting, a lovely old man who worked in a clothing store across the street and had known me since I was a little girl, came up to see me. When he kissed me and said "Good luck," I had a hard time not crying. Something about him reminded me of my father, from whom I would not be getting a good-luck kiss that day.

It was a 45-minute drive to the church, and at 7:15 Adolfo and Mother left. In Argentina the groom and all the other participants arrive at the time the wedding is scheduled. The bride and her escort arrive thirty minutes later. So we had half an hour to wait, my cousin and I. The maids all came to wish me well. And I walked around the big apartment once more.

Then my cousin said, "It's time to go." Suddenly I was terrified. Did I really want to get married? "Don't be ridiculous," I replied. "You are married already." When I went down the stairs, everyone was there to see me off. Strangers on the sidewalk and in cars stopped to cry "Good luck!" and "God bless you!"

All the way to the church people recognized the bridal car and waved and shouted greetings. I was touched and grateful. How seldom in life humans seem really to care for one another.

As we approached the church, I began to get nervous. My cousin talked to me about the United States, our school in St. Louis, anything to keep my mind off myself. At the door of the church, we got out. Someone straightened at my dress and tried to get me to smile. The man in charge of the procession was told that we were ready. An assistant was sent to ring the church bell three times to let the congregation know that the procession was about to begin. My cousin offered me his arm.

Then all at once the giant doors of the cathedral swung open, the lights in the church went on, and 1500 people stood up and turned around to face me. As the great organ began to play, I felt my cousin step forward. The wedding had begun. Far away I saw Monsignor Auletta at the altar, my mother-in-law, my brother-in-law, and, of course, Bruno. Before I knew it, tears of joy were running down my cheeks. For a moment I worried about my make-up. But what difference could it made at a time like this?

As we approached the altar, Bruno came, took my hand and escorted me the rest of the way. All through the ceremony the tears continued to run down my face. We exchanged rings and were declared man and wife. Then we knelt together as Marta Benegas, one of Argentina's great opera singers, sang Schubert's "Ave Maria." I looked up at the Virgin on the altar. Marta had said that she would have to look away from me while she sang or she would begin to cry herself. As she sang the last Ave Maria I heard her voice falter, and I knew she had looked.

Finally Monsignor Auletta read a telegram of blessing from His Holiness Pope Paul and spoke of Bruno's and my love for music and our plans to make a start in a new country. He asked God's blessing on our lives and on the children we would have. His little talk reminded me that the story wouldn't end with the wedding—that it would go on and on. As we turned to leave the altar, Mendelssohn's "Wedding March" boomed out from the organ's huge pipes and we took our first steps together as man and wife.

19

THE DAY after our wedding, we left Buenos Aires for Mar del Plata, where the Bottazzis had loaned us an apartment for our honeymoon. Our stay there was a short but happy one, except for the first shock of married life: I had to do the dishes. Never in my life had I had to wash dishes and I hated it!

When it finally came time for us to depart for the United States, everyone came to the airport to see us off. Bruno and I were glad to be on our way, but we were also each a little scared. Just before we boarded the plane, one of Bruno's family said to him, "We'll expect a telegram asking for money within a month." At the time we didn't know what a problem money would turn out to be, and we laughed; but for years afterward whenever we were depressed and began thinking of returning to Argentina, we remembered this remark and found strength to stay a little longer and try a little harder.

132   On the plane Bruno and I were both very

low. Tears were streaming down our cheeks as we waved for the last time. But once we were aloft and headed north, our spirits began to improve. We ordered drinks to celebrate our new undertaking and began to look ahead. Of course we were a little crazy to be starting out for a new country without even knowing the language, but we were confident of our abilities and knew we'd survive.

The next day we arrived in New York. Since we were immigrants and not just tourists, the customs officials made us wait until everyone else had gone through the line. But then we were admitted to the United States as permanent residents. One of the papers of welcome touched us deeply. It was printed in several languages, including Spanish, and said, No matter what country you come from, you need never feel foreign here since this country is made up of people from every part of the world. It went on to suggest that if a new immigrant didn't like the United States he might consider returning to his own country rather than speaking against America.

This may seem harsh to people who have lived here all their lives. But Bruno and I now love this country, and few things make us angrier than when other immigrants, most of whom are living far better here than they ever did "at home," complain about their lot here.

Our first day in the United States we had to go from Kennedy Airport to a Wall Street bank in order to get our money from Argentina. Argentine law prohibited us from taking more than $400 apiece out of the country and we couldn't even carry that with us. Our trip into New York was a nightmare. We got lost over and over and even began to wonder if we would get our money in time to catch the plane to St. Louis. Yet finally we caught the bus to LaGuardia Airport and were able to relax and to look around. That short ride has stayed with us ever since. Everything seemed so big—not only the skyscrapers, but the cars, the highways, even the airport.

In St. Louis we were met by the Chabays, who had been so helpful in making arrangements for us with the university. And our first meal was hot dogs which I love and had begged for. However, we soon learned that it was a good thing we didn't expect to eat steak at every meal. Bruno's assistantship was not being awarded because all conducting courses for the year had been cancelled. This left Bruno with little to do and the two of us with an income after taxes of only $180 a month. To make matters worse, I discovered at the end of October that I was pregnant, and though Bruno immediately began looking for work, his poor English was a severe handicap.

Many nights we ate spaghetti flavored with a little butter and some A-1 steak sauce.

Yet we still laugh at many small things which happened that year. One Sunday Bruno went to a local store for milk and a newspaper. It wasn't open yet, and he couldn't understand it—the store was always open by that time on Sundays. Of course it turned out that that was the weekend daylight savings time switched to standard time. But we had never heard of such a thing and no one had thought to tell us.

Not long afterward we got up one Thursday to find *everything* closed—stores, banks, even the university. We wondered if they had decided to set the calendar back a day just as they had set the clocks back by an hour. But toward noon our landlady brought us a beautiful turkey just out of the oven and explained that it was Thanksgiving, a national holiday. We were grateful to her for the wonderful bird—and happy to know that we weren't going crazy.

There was also the day Bruno needed a haircut. Since neither of us spoke much English, we went to the barbershop together. While we were waiting Bruno saw a sign on the wall that he thought must be the English for haircut. When his turn came, the barber nodded and said, "Hello, how are you?"   135

Bruno pointed to his head and replied, "Keep smiling."

The barber rephrased the question, and Bruno again pointed to his head and said, "Keep smiling." The barber finally understood when Bruno pointed to the sign. But it was months before we realized how puzzled the barber must have been.

Shortly after Christmas we moved into a smaller, less expensive apartment, but money was still a serious concern and I was beginning to feel worse and worse. I was taking a full load of courses toward an American masters degree and teaching piano at the university, but even the busy life and my condition didn't explain why I was so weak and exhausted. One day I fainted in class, then I began doing so regularly. Together with this, I had morning sickness from the first week of pregnancy until five minutes before I entered the delivery room. Why Bruno didn't simply walk out I shall never know.

My obstetrician couldn't find out what was wrong with me. One day in the spring he took Bruno aside and said, "Your child is very healthy, but I'm not sure your wife will live long enough to deliver." He wanted to put me in the hospital for a series of tests, but we decided to seek the opinion of a second doctor first.

Bruno and I were directed to a young Italian obstetrician who, after a simple blood test, told me I was dangerously anemic. He gave me a shot of iron right there, and then another each day for two weeks. I soon felt like new.

Nevertheless, we thought we should go back to Argentina before the baby was due. First, expenses would be less by almost enough to pay our airfare. Second, I wanted to be near Mother when our first child was born. Our doctor advised me that I should fly no later than five weeks before the baby was due. So I had to apply to the university to take my examinations early. All my teachers were most helpful and cooperative except one—the man with whom I was studying piano. I knew why.

That April, a group called the Artists' Presentation Society was to hold its annual competition for St. Louis musicians. I wanted to enter. "Oh no," my teacher said. "You're not ready, not prepared for such a thing."

I considered my long experience in such events and decided to enter anyway. The early stages went well and I got to the finals. Of course I was seven months pregnant by now and looked more like nine months, but I came out on the stage as gracefully as I could under the circumstances. After my other pieces were finished, I launched into

"Malambo," by my old teacher in Argentina, Alberto Ginastera, an exciting piece full of Latin American rhythms that had been a favorite of mine for years. As I hit the first big chord, however, I felt the piano roll away from me. Apparently no one had locked its wheels. At the first opportunity, I slid up closer on the stool; but then when I hit another chord the piano rolled once again. All through the piece the piano rolled and I scooted after it. I kept expecting the judges to stop me since in this kind of competition they seldom hear a piece all the way through.

Whether they were enchanted by my playing or fascinated by the sight of a pregnant woman chasing a grand piano across the stage, they didn't stop me. And by the time the piece was over, half the piano was no longer visible from the floor, while the keyboard and I were against the curtain.

Still, I won the competition, $200 and a chance to play a recital. The money was welcome and I was happy to play a recital for all those who had been so kind to us in St. Louis, but my piano teacher was furious because I had entered and had won.

When Bruno and I left for Buenos Aires, we had already decided not to return to St. Louis. The year had not been a happy one. Bruno had been idle most of the time, we had been very short of money, and I had been sick. But I suspect the major problem was that we were making so many adjustments at once—learning to live together, learning a new language, getting used to a new country, and preparing to become parents. We were happy to be going "home" for a visit.

✑ 20

AFTER our baby was born we planned to return to the United States. I had applied to play in the Van Cliburn competition in Texas in September; then we had decided to go to New York and make a life for ourselves there as musicians. New York is the musical capital of the world, more exciting and dynamic than Paris or Vienna could ever be. With such big plans, we never considered that our troubles in St. Louis were only a preparation for more to come.

We arrived in Buenos Aires in May and the baby was due in June. But June ran out and July began, and still no baby. By this time I was huge, too big to stand for more than a few minutes at a time. Finally, toward the middle of July, I was confined to bed.

On Friday, July 15, I received a call from a good friend, Mercedes Molina Anchorena, who had also been a close friend of Monsignor Franceschi, and suddenly I was drawn back into the past.

*   *   *

From the time of that first cruise to Europe when I was thirteen, I had remained in constant touch with Monsignor Franceschi. In Paris he came to see us at least once a year and when he was in Buenos Aires we wrote each other regularly. During my vacations from the Conservatory, I was in Buenos Aires and would visit the Monsignor twice a week.

Shortly after my eighteenth birthday I returned to Argentina permanently. During my first year home Monsignor Franceschi spent time in jail at the hands of the Peron regime and we all were worried about him. One day after his release Mercedes Molina Anchorena and I were together in the Monsignor's office. She was a member of one of Argentina's most prominent families and had been a newspaper correspondent in several countries. She was also very active in religious affairs and it was she who would obtain the personal blessing of Pope Paul that was read at our wedding. That day, the Monsignor said to her, "Mercedes, when I am dead and gone, I want you to take care of my friend Ana Maria if she should ever need your help." She promised and that was that.

During my second year of study in Buenos Aires, Monsignor Franceschi collapsed while addressing a church meeting in Montevideo,

Uruguay. Immediately I took a plane to be with him. I spent hours at his bedside in Montevideo even though he was seldom conscious. After a week, my father came to take me home. When I went back in to say goodbye to my friend, I had a presentiment that I would never see him again in this life. As I sat there he opened his eyes and saw me. "You are a very good human being," he said. Then he made the sign of the cross. "God bless you." He closed his eyes and his hand fell to his side.

For the next few days I was in a state of acute anxiety. I couldn't concentrate on anything, even a casual conversation. Then on Thursday night, July 11, I was fixing my hair and all at once I felt calm and relaxed for the first time since the Monsignor had become ill. A few minutes later Mercedes Molina Anchorena called me to say that the Monsignor had just died.

Then came the grief. For three months I was beside myself. I lay about unable to do anything but eat and sleep. I gained 30 pounds and refused to see anyone. I wanted to die. My parents were unable to shake me out of my withdrawal. Then one day Mercedes Molina Anchorena called me. She said she understood how I felt, but she refused to pity me. "If you don't feel like living anymore," she said, "take a gun and shoot yourself. But if you continue this way, you will kill your parents as well as yourself, and you have no right to do that."

Before Monsignor Franceschi's death I had scheduled a recital that was coming up soon. Since I hadn't practiced for weeks, I told everyone the recital would have to be canceled. Now Mercedes asked me please to play. "Nothing would have pleased the Monsignor more," she said. I gave her no satisfaction during that long call, still refusing to do anything. But her words had reached me. The next morning I got up and without saying a word to anyone sat down to practice. And I played the recital.

Now that same Mercedes Molina Anchorena was calling me again. "Listen," she said. "Tomorrow is the name day of the Virgin of Carmelo. You remember how devoted the Monsignor was to the Carmelite order. Promise me that if you give birth tomorrow and have a son you will name him Gustavo after Gustave Franceschi." Contrary to the strong custom in Italian families that the first son be named after his father, I agreed.

That night at 7:30 I went into labor and was rushed to the hospital. Eighteen hours later, on July 16, after a difficult delivery, our son

Gustavo was born, weighing eleven pounds three ounces.

Shortly after our return home I began to hemorrhage, and a day later I had lost so much blood that I was taken back to the hospital. At four the same afternoon I went into shock; several times the doctors thought I was past saving, but after massive transfusions the bleeding finally slowed to a trickle. By Saturday, a week from the delivery, I had improved so much that I was told I could go home the next day.

Then at 10:30 that night it started all over again. My doctor was not available, and the interns refused to take me seriously. They said they would be playing cards up on the next floor if I needed anything. I could feel my strength ebbing away.

In desperation, I called my father. I had not spoken to him since three months before our wedding and I was afraid he might not even talk to me. When he heard my voice, he was very cold.

"What do you want?" he asked.

"Father, I am dying," I said. Speaking quickly because I was afraid I would lose consciousness, I told him my situation.

"I'll call you back in ten minutes," he said.

Sooner than that the telephone rang. "My friend Dr. Bensadon, is on the way."

When Dr. Bensadon arrived, he examined me, asked a few questions and tried without success to get my record of treatment. Then he told me that he must operate immediately to determine the cause of the bleeding. There was only one problem: although he was a well-known gynecologist, he didn't have operating privileges at that hospital. I heard him arguing with the hospital administrator. His voice grew louder and louder, but the administrator refused him permission to operate. Only when Dr. Bensadon threatened to call the police did the official back down.

The operation began at midnight. I remember seeing the clock in the operating room just before Dr. Bensadon said, "I'm going to put you to sleep now, but don't worry. I shall not leave your side until you are out of danger."

The next thing I remember it was 4 o'clock. Dr. Bensadon had discovered that the doctors had failed to remove part of the placenta after Gustavo's birth. Then just as the operation was concluding, I went into shock and my blood pressure began to plummet.

I could see the whole thing as if I were watching from a corner of the room near the ceiling. Dr. Bensadon is more and more distraught as a technician reads out my blood pressure: "Five . . . four . . . three . . ." Several people are trying desperately to find a vein 145 that is not collapsed so they can start a transfusion. Dr. Bensadon takes a scalpel and cuts into my leg near the ankle. He pulls out two veins and connects them for the transfusion. The blood begins to flow, but he sends a doctor to the waiting room to tell Bruno that I am near death. Then I slip into unconsciousness once again.

When I went to visit Dr. Bensadon for a final examination a few weeks later, he said, "I don't know what your religion is or to whom you pray. But you should be grateful for your life. By all human standards you should be dead."

21

ON AUGUST 15, Gustavo was baptized by Monsignor Auletta, the same priest who had married Bruno and me a year earlier, and Mercedes Molina Anchorena was his godmother. Shortly thereafter we returned to the United States in time for the Cliburn festival. We flew to Miami, where we had to go through customs and change planes for Dallas-Fort Worth. Oh, how tired we were! Gustavo was fussing, we had dozens of pieces of luggage, and the lines seemed endless.

Our flight to Texas that day was terrifying. Almost from the moment we took off, the plane was tossed about like a toy. We had to keep our seatbelts on, the stewardesses couldn't serve dinner and Gustavo cried the whole way. When we finally landed safely in Texas, I breathed a huge sigh of relief.

We were met at the airport by a young woman who was to be our hostess during the competition. She and her husband took us in, babysat and helped me find a place to practice. 147

I knew that I had no chance to win because I had not been able to practice since I left St. Louis. I was just hoping not to embarrass myself. I was tired and my memory kept playing its old tricks.

In the first round I played poorly and lost all chance to finish well. But I still had to stay until the whole competition was over. Well before then, however, our hosts were tired of us, and I can't blame them. They had agreed to put up a pianist, not a whole family. Finally the husband called the competition headquarters and said that because his wife was ill they couldn't keep us any longer. We packed our things and he drove us down to the office. There we sat while a woman tried to find someone else who would take us for the last week. We were miserable.

At last a Mrs. Harry Logan, Jr., came to our rescue. From the moment Mrs. Logan delivered the little Bottazzi band up to her door, she treated us as her own son and daughter. She helped with the baby, fed us wonderful meals, and took care of all arrangements with the competition committee. She even paid for a call to Buenos Aires so that I could talk to Mother.

The day of our departure for New York was approaching. We had arranged to go by bus to save money. Mrs. Logan made sandwiches and gathered up all the things we would need for our trip. Her daughter, who had a one-year-old child, contributed a hundred jars of baby food for Gustavo though he was still too young to eat it. When Mrs. Logan saw us off at the bus station, I felt I was saying a last farewell to a dear friend.

The bus ride seemed to last forever. For two days and nights we rode, trading Gustavo back and forth and trying to find comfortable ways for all three of us to sleep. Halfway through the trip I ran out of formula for Gustavo and didn't know what to do. So I bought plain cow's milk when we stopped and fed that to him. Immediately he began throwing up. It was not a happy time.

Finally, on the morning of October 18, 1966, we saw the skyline of New York City approaching. This was not the kind of arrival I had dreamed about. We were exhausted and unwashed. We had a sick baby and no friends, little money and no jobs. In fact, we hardly knew what to do next.

We checked our baggage and walked outside the terminal. It was cold and rainy as we wandered through the streets, staring up at the huge buildings and looking for a place to stay. Every time we stopped at a hotel it was an effort for both of us. Our English was still not good, and we were afraid that people wouldn't understand us. The first dozen hotels we tried were full, and we were getting colder and wetter all the time. Now the skyscrapers didn't seem so inspiring. They just made us feel small and insignificant.

At last we found a hotel. The room was horribly expensive, but we didn't care any more. It was warm and it was safe. We left Gustavo on the bed asleep and ran all the way back to the bus station to get our luggage. When we returned in a taxi, the manager of the hotel was waiting for us. Gustavo had awakened, and someone had reported his crying. When the manager discovered him to be alone in the room, he was furious. He told us that if this ever happened again, he would throw us out. We apologized as best we could and went up to our room.

How wonderful that bed looked after two nights on the bus! Bruno and I took showers. Then we lay down and fell asleep. During the next twenty-four hours we got up only to look after the baby.

✂ 22

NOW BEGAN our most serious trial. Every morning we bought the papers and went through the help-wanted ads. At first we were determined to get jobs in music. But there were very few such positions and those few didn't match our qualifications. We visited a number of music schools, but it was October and their teachers had already been hired for the year.

As the days went by, our money supply became smaller and smaller. Obviously we couldn't wait to find musical jobs, so we began to consider what else we might do. To begin with, we would have to move out of our hotel as soon as possible.

Through a South American acquaintance, we found an apartment in Forest Hills, a 30-minute subway ride from Manhattan. Early in November we moved in. It was a two-family house; we had two rooms on the main floor and three more downstairs in the basement. Now at least we could fix our own food and reduce our expenses for rent. But the trip to the city to look for jobs was longer, and we had to leave Gustavo with a babysitter.

By mid-November we had gone to every employment agency in town and filled out hundreds of forms. We were willing to take any honest work, but the agents and interviewers seemed skeptical. If we told them about our backgrounds in music, they thought we were too good for low-paying jobs. If we didn't tell them, they complained about our poor English and lack of office skills. Little by little we learned what they wanted to hear, and that's what we told them. We didn't like lying, but we had to eat and our money was running out.

One day I became so frustrated that I wrote a letter to Governor Nelson Rockefeller explaining our problems. A week later we got a response from his office suggesting that we go to the State Employment Office. When we showed this letter to the people there, they were eager to help and after hours of checking, finally thought they had jobs for us. The positions were as "house parents" to a group of fifteen delinquent boys. Bruno and I were so desperate that we considered accepting. But how could we, with our small baby and poor English, live in a kind of prison with fifteen difficult teenagers? Finally we said no.

Then we heard of another opportunity. A big department store was looking for Christmas help. We applied and were accepted. I was to work in the overdue accounts department and Bruno was to work in the warehouse. For a few minutes we were happy. Then they told us the salary—$55 a week for each of us before taxes and other deductions. We did some quick figuring and concluded that after paying our transportation, babysitting and rent, we would have nothing left to pay for food. In the meantime we wouldn't even be able to look for other jobs. So we walked out.

In December we received a check from my father "to buy toys for Gustavo for Christmas"—God bless him!—which of course went for food and rent. We had written our families the second week we were in New York and told them we had jobs and were happy, not daring to tell the truth. After what Bruno's family had said we'd have done almost anything before we asked for help.

Christmas was not a happy one. There were a few toys for Gustavo, and a small piece of meat for Bruno and me. True, we had lived poorly in St. Louis just the year before, but neither of us had ever lived as poorly as this. And there seemed to be no end in sight.

Tramping from one interview to the next,

worrying where our next dollar would come from, all I could think of was how much money I had seen and spent in my life. Money talks, I had often heard people say. But poverty is silent and desperate.

I had always thought Mother was the one in our family with extrasensory perception. But in January, when another check arrived from Father, I changed my mind. Once again, it came just in time. We had been reduced to potatoes for us and milk for Gustavo. Fortunately, we had the baby food that had been given us in Texas. Sometimes I was so hungry that I hoped Gustavo would leave a little in the bottom of one of those jars for me to finish.

Still we answered the advertisements, made the rounds of the employment agencies and as the dismal winter dragged on, Bruno and I hardly dared mention our discouragement to each other.

Then one day in February an agency called to say that it had arranged interviews for us at two different Wall Street banks. My interview was scheduled for Thursday and Bruno's for Friday. I went without much enthusiasm since I had been through so many interviews without any result. But this time the interviewer seemed interested in my languages and to my utter astonishment I was offered the job. It

paid $360 a month and I was to start the fol-
lowing day.

The next morning, after leaving Gustavo
with a babysitter, Bruno and I went to Wall
Street, I to start work and he to go to his
interview. When we met for lunch he said
that he was to start work Tuesday.

That Saturday we celebrated with a leg of
lamb—real meat—for dinner. In my excitement I slipped and fell. Right away I knew
something had happened to my ankle, but I
finished the meal before I lay down to rest it.
Though the ankle swelled and hurt terribly, I
kept telling myself that it was only a sprain.
Monday was a holiday, so with an extra day
to rest it, I would get up and go to work on
Tuesday as if nothing had happened.

On Tuesday, the only shoe that would fit
me was one of Bruno's and I had a cane to help
carry my weight. We set off for Manhattan an
hour earlier than we had planned. It took half
an hour to walk to the subway and then the
real trip began—dragging myself up and
down endless stairs, being pushed and
shoved, watching the time slip by. Needless to
say, I was terrified that if I didn't show up for
work I would lose my job. When I finally
arrived ten minutes after the hour, my boss
glared at me and said, "You're late." When
she saw my leg, however, she came right over 155

to ask what was wrong. "Nothing," I said. I was afraid she would fire me on the spot. But she wasn't fooled; she could see that I was in pain and she said that I would have to visit the doctor. I began to cry. Bruno and I had twelve dollars between us to last until Friday when we got our first paychecks.

My boss arranged for me to see a doctor in the same building; and he agreed to wait for payment until the end of the week. She sent a Colombian who worked for the bank up to the doctor with me so that he could translate. The doctor took X rays and examined my ankle. Then I learned the worst.

"You have two fractures," he told me, "and they are serious. You have aggravated the injury by walking on it. The bones must be set and your leg should be in traction. That means you must stay in the hospital for about a week and then in bed for six weeks more."

I can't believe it, I thought to myself. How can I go to the hospital? I have a six-month-old baby to care for and no money at all. If I go, Bruno will have to stay home and care for the baby and he will lose his job, too. No matter how I figured, I couldn't see how we'd avoid disaster. I told the doctor I had to speak to my husband and would call him that evening.

That night, through a friend, we learned of

Dr. Alexander de la Garza. He was from Mexico and practiced near our apartment in Forest Hills. When I spoke to him on the telephone he seemed very understanding and told me to meet him the next morning at Flushing Hospital.

After examining me the following day, Dr. de la Garza said that if I was willing to have my ankle set without anesthesia in the emergency room it would be much less expensive. And he would allow me to recuperate at home if I promised to stay in bed for the first six weeks. He said there was the possibility my ankle would have to be rebroken and reset later even if I did stay off it. The next six weeks were hard for us all. I had Gustavo from 7:30 in the morning until 6:30 at night on weekdays. Then when Bruno came home he had to cook, clean up and get us all off to bed. With only one salary, we had no money either. There was one positive note: my employer had agreed to hold my job until I could return.

During those weeks all I could do was ask myself where had we gone wrong. Ever since our marriage it seemed that Bruno and I had staggered from one disaster to another. His difficulties in St. Louis, mine in Buenos Aires, our nightmare months in New York. Then, just when we had found jobs, this broken ankle. There was a piano in the apartment, but since St. Louis I don't believe I had played it for more than a few minutes at a time. When I flew home to have Gustavo, I had dreamed that I would return to the United States to win the Cliburn competition. Then Bruno and I would march triumphantly into a New York that was waiting for us with open arms. But things had turned out somewhat differently.

23

APRIL 1967. It has been five years since I returned to Buenos Aires after the accident. Now I am a clerk for the French-American Bank in New York City. I hobble to work each day with a cast on my foot. I am married, and my husband and I between us earn $8000 a year before taxes. Our son, who is now eight months old, spends five days a week with a babysitter. The piano is beginning to seem a distant memory as I have not been in real performing condition since I left Tokyo two and a half years ago.

The only thing that kept Bruno and me sane was our dream of returning to music. Passing Carnegie Hall in our travels around New York we would stop to look at the posters announcing forthcoming appearances. Someday, we told each other, *our* names will be up there. These dreams took a very specific form. On our second night out together in Buenos Aires we had heard Rachmaninoff's Second Piano Concerto. We adopted this wonderfully romantic piece as our own and decided that when we played in Carnegie Hall, this would be one of the selections. Bruno would conduct and I would be the soloist. This dream has never entirely left us.

The Wall Street job soon became suffocating. I worked in a big room full of clerks without any windows. We couldn't tell whether it was rainy or clear without peeking through someone's office. And our supervisors treated us as machines rather than as people.

Every day Bruno and I would meet at lunch and commiserate, as our jobs were much the same. We'd share a chocolate milkshake, return to work, meet again at five o'clock, get Gustavo and travel home by subway.

Before April was over, something happened that improved our spirits immensely. A Miss Thode called from the Bronx Institute for the Education of the Blind. In January, when we were still looking for jobs, we responded to a want ad for a music teacher in the Bronx. After our interviews there had been an audition. I played badly, so badly in fact that Bruno was angry. "You could have played a little better," he said sourly as we left. Miss Thode, who was chairman of the music department, had thanked us and that had been that.

Now she was on the phone asking if we

were still interested in the jobs. There were two, one fulltime and one parttime, available in September. Both Bruno and I were wild with excitement but managed to restrain ourselves. Yes, we said, we would be interested. She explained that teachers were required to live in apartments on the school grounds and a two-bedroom apartment came with the jobs. Would we object to that? Looking around our basement kitchen and remembering the long winter we had just spent there, we said we wouldn't mind at all. So Miss Thode suggested that we come up the following week, see the apartment and sign our contracts if we decided to take the jobs. The next moment Bruno and I were jumping up and down. Just the prospect of working in music again made life exciting.

A week later Bruno and I visited the Bronx. When we saw the apartment we couldn't wait to move in. It was on the ground floor, it had windows, and there was even a small yard in the back. We signed the contracts.

May dragged by ever so slowly. Of course in one respect we were much happier, having something to look forward to, but now the days at the bank seemed longer than ever. My ankle was a continuing problem. It did not heal properly and in April I had needed hospital treatment. We were in no position to pay for this and, once again, Mrs. Logan of Texas came to our rescue, loaning us the money which she later turned into a gift. In June, after nearly four months, my cast came off. At last I was free!

July 15—the day we were to move to the Bronx—finally arrived. It was a Saturday, and we persuaded a friend to bring his station wagon to Forest Hills to pick up our things. We barely managed to stuff it all into his car. How had we collected so many possessions on so little money?

When we got to the Bronx, however, we began to realize how many things we were missing. The first time we had seen the apartment it was furnished with someone else's furniture. Now it was bare. We had neither table nor chairs, no living room furniture, not even a bed for Bruno and me. We were embarrassed to ask for a bed, but finally did and the Institute found two right away. They were narrow and not very comfortable, but they were better than the floor and we were grateful.

We woke up that first morning in our new apartment and had a delicious breakfast in the middle of the living room floor. Gustavo was one year old that day, and we invited a few friends over for an Argentine-style barbeque in the back yard. As the meat roasted Bruno and I lifted our wine glasses in a silent toast to each other. After the many trials of the past year, our lives appeared to be on the rise.

We had decided to leave the bank two weeks before our teaching jobs began, as we couldn't afford to leave any sooner than that. Now with five weeks to go every day was agony. In August we gave our notice. And finally, on August 24, we took Gustavo to the babysitter's and traveled to Wall Street for the last time. At lunch that day Bruno and I met as usual, but instead of sharing a milkshake, we went to a Mexican restaurant for chicken and rice, our first real weekday meal since we started work.

For the next two weeks we sat in our small back yard and relaxed. After our first eleven months in the United States we felt we deserved a short vacation. We had picked up enough furniture to make the apartment livable, and soon we began to regard the little house with tender affection. We had found a home.

24

ON SEPTEMBER 4 school opened and Miss Thode gave me keys to the class building and to my studio. "This is your room," she said. "You have the key and you may use it any time of the day or night." What lovely words—and what a beautiful studio! There were two pianos, an upright and a Steinway "B" grand. The window looked out across Pelham Parkway toward trees and grass. Not until those first weeks with a piano and time to practice did I fully appreciate how much I had missed music.

Our early months at the Institute were an education for Bruno and me. At first I was ill-at-ease with my young students. But I soon came to admire their ability to get along in the world and their complete lack of self-pity. They could recognize you in the hall just by the way you walked. Some were fine musicians. And there were even things the pianists could do better than pianists with sight. For instance, they seldom missed the long jump from the middle register to a high register because they relied on their muscles to tell them where to land. People who depend on their eyes often make mistakes.

Bruno began the year with a parttime appointment. But in November he was given fulltime duties and suddenly we had 25 percent more money coming in. The first thing we did was to buy the best dishwasher on the market. Ever since the second morning of our marriage I had hated dishes and now at last I could pass the job on. We also began to look for a car, and by the end of the month purchased one on time payments.

Best of all, however, was being able to return to the piano in a serious way. I started way back at the beginning—almost as far back as I had just after the accident. Once more I got out the Burgmüller and my other beginning studies. Little by little I began to improve.

As well as teaching piano, I was instructing three classes in general music. This gave me a big chance to improve my English and to play in front of an audience again.

At first I just played excerpts to illustrate points about keys, cadences, musical structure and other topics we studied. But soon I was preparing a "program" for one day each week. During my years there I played entire sonatas by Mozart, Haydn, Beethoven, Schubert, Schumann, Brahms, and Liszt. Planning to play for class forced me to review all this music carefully and though I never tried playing anything from memory, I did learn to play reasonably well again.

By spring I was so encouraged by my progress that I began to think about performing again before a larger public. And when I learned the famous Busoni competition was to be held in Italy early that fall, I decided to enter.

But even before Bruno and I made our reservations I began to see that I was pushing myself too hard. My memory was just not up to it. I hadn't tried to memorize anything since the year after the accident when I had the strange experience with *Kreisleriana,* playing by memory one day and discovering that I couldn't remember a note the next. In Tokyo and St. Louis I had done most of my playing with music but now, memorizing new music and keeping up with everything else simply proved too much. So I wrote to Italy and cancelled my application to perform.

It was a depressing setback and I went into one of my rages. Ninety-nine percent of the people on earth get along just fine without playing the piano, I told myself. And so I
closed my piano one day and resolved never

to play again except for classwork or pleasure. But I soon realized that I couldn't simply run away. I am a pianist whether I like it or not. Playing is part of me, and no small disappointment will ever change that fact. Despite the cancellation, Bruno and I finished our first year at the Institute in better spirits than we had known since our marriage.

In the fall of 1968, our second at the Institute, we also began teaching at a branch of the Brooklyn Conservatory of Music. Twice a week we would drive to Queens and give half-hour lessons to private students. These students varied widely in their abilities and in their degree of seriousness. They were neither as precocious as the ones I had taught in Paris nor as single-minded in their eagerness to please as those in Tokyo. Talking to our new students and their parents, we discovered that most children who took piano lessons were involved in half a dozen activities at the same time: ballet on Monday, Girl Scouts on Tuesday, church group on Wednesday, and so on. When I suggested to the parents of the more gifted students that their children might be better off concentrating on one or two activities, most of them didn't seem to agree—although they often promised to try to get their son or daughter to practice a little more. We slowly learned that for many Americans being "well rounded" is more important than doing any single thing well. Even with a bright student such an attitude guarantees failure. To be fair, our better pupils were often very imaginative and indeed wanted to be good musicians. But too often they were simply not willing to put in the long hours of hard work that were necessary. It's amazing how much talent one sees in a year of teaching—and it's sad how little of that talent is ever fully developed. Some of our students at the Institute who had fewer opportunities were able to accomplish more with less talent than our private students.

Of course some talent is required to be a good performing musician. But willpower and a sense of discipline are also important. These qualities had been drilled into me before I was twelve years old. I remember hating the way Mother forced me to practice and never let me give up until I had perfected the passage or piece I was playing.

Now, years later, I'm grateful to her for having pushed me so hard. And I believe that other children would benefit if their parents pushed them a little harder to do something really well.

❧ 25

JUST after Thanksgiving that year I received a letter from Buenos Aires. The message was brief: "If you want to see your father again, come soon. He is dying."

At first I didn't want to believe it. My father had been close to death many times yet had always recovered. Why should this be any different? But I also knew that he had cancer and had been receiving treatments for the last nine years. He was no longer young. I decided that we should go.

There was one big obstacle. We had no money, and round-trip air fare to Argentina for the three of us was $1700. We had one credit card with a $200 borrowing limit, and I was so desperate I decided to go to the airline office, make the reservations and offer the card. They could only say no.

The clerk was unfamiliar with the card and went off to see her supervisor. I paced up and down, praying things would work out. I loved my father; and I begged God to let me see him one more time. The clerk returned with a big smile. The charge had been approved!

I cried, as usual, when we landed on Argentine soil; and I guess I always will. Then I called my father, who was at home (as is the custom there) even though he was mortally ill. He answered and sounded wonderful. How could he be dying? But then he told me himself. And when I saw him there seemed little question. He was so thin.

We spent two weeks in Buenos Aires, traveling between our apartment, where Mother still lived, and my father's house. Even though we both knew this would be our last visit, he and I could still not resist fighting—almost as if for old time's sake.

The final evening of our stay, Bruno and Gustavo wished my father farewell. Then I went in to say good-bye. When I saw he was reading a newspaper, I was furious. I was not even going to kiss him, but Bruno insisted. When I bent down, I saw that the newspaper was upside down and that Father's eyes were filled with tears.

I went to kiss him on the cheek, afraid that if we embraced I would break down altogether. But he reached out and we held each other close for a moment. When I got to the door I looked back at him once more, to re-

170 member.

Next morning at the airport, just before boarding, I called my father one last time. I could tell from his voice that he was under heavy sedation, but he knew me and we said our last goodbye.

Three weeks later, as I was leaving my studio one night, I thought I saw my father's reflection in the glass door. I was terrified and hurried downstairs to where Bruno was waiting for me. As we walked to our apartment a block away I told him what I had seen and he managed to calm me. But then on top of the mail box I saw a telegram. I knew what it said before I even picked it up.

Even though I had not been close to Father for some time and even though we had hurt each other terribly over the years, he was certainly the most important man in my life. And when he died I lost something precious—a feeling of security, a belief that no matter how bad things might be between us, he would reach out to help me if I was in trouble.

Father never quite approved of my being a pianist. He once told me, "If you want to travel around the world, you don't have to go as a musician." But still, I wanted to be like him, to make something of myself by myself.

That winter Bruno began having excruciating pains in his back. Some days he could walk no more than a few steps. The doctors weren't sure what was wrong. All they would say was that he should stay flat in bed for a month or two, but for people in our situation that was impossible. We needed both our incomes to make ends meet—and to pay the angry credit company for our trip to Argentina. Yet we limped along through the rest of the school year as I continued to play for my students and practice whenever I could. Bruno finally visited Dr. de la Garza, who had been so helpful when I broke my ankle. Once again, the good doctor seemed to know what to do and Bruno gradually recovered.

The fall of 1969 was our third at the Institute, and by now Bruno and I were becoming restless. However good it had been to us, we had no intention of making our careers there. For one thing, our private teaching took up an increasing part of our time. And we wanted to begin to move toward our ultimate goals— mine as a pianist and Bruno's as a conductor.

That fall we decided to go back to school one more time. I had not completed my work at Washington University and Bruno had not been able to study there at all. We wrote for catalogs and applied to several schools with good music programs. Though we planned to continue our private teaching, we would require some financial assistance.

By January the choice was between Yale and the State University of New York at Stony Brook. We visited both campuses and fell in love with Stony Brook, a new campus on eastern Long Island about 60 miles from New York City. Yale offered us assistantships and is the more prestigious of the two schools. But we didn't feel nearly as much "at home" there, and we agreed that if Stony Book offered us some financial help we would go there. While we were making our decision, I got a letter from Argentina that was to haunt me for some time to come. Raul Sieiro, my mother's brother and a favorite uncle of mine, wrote to congratulate us on our plans to go back to school. But he went on to remind me that all my early training had been to prepare me for the concert stage and that he hoped I wouldn't give up this dream.

In February Bruno went out to Stony Brook for an audition and came home joyous. He had been offered an assistantship to the conductor of the university orchestra. The next day I was to audition at the New York apartment of Martin Canin, chairman of the piano department at Stony Brook and a member of the faculty at the Juilliard School of Music. If I was successful, our way to Stony Brook would be assured.

Bruno drove me to Manhattan the follow- 173

ing morning. I was as nervous as could be. For two years I had not played except for my students at the Institute. Now I would be playing for musicians who would recognize every error. I have always had trouble playing well for other musicians, perhaps because Mother used to sit beside me for hours on end and point out every mistake I made. Once she became so impatient that she slapped my face every time I slipped up.

I didn't play as well as I might have that day, but Mr. Canin offered me a fellowship— a scholarship for which no work need be done. And soon Mr. Canin, for whom I was to develop great respect and admiration became the driving force in my campaign to really play again.

Miss Thode was very surprised when she heard we wouldn't be returning that fall. I believe she thought we had settled in forever. A few days before school ended, the students and teachers gave us a wonderful party, presenting Bruno an elegant pair of gold cufflinks and me earrings with pearls set in gold.

26

WE MOVED to Stony Brook at the end of June. This time we rented a real house just across the street from the university and for this move we needed a large van to transport all our possessions.

Stony Brook, a small town set in quiet countryside, seemed wonderful to us. The University is new, and its beautiful buildings and thousands of students gave the place an excitement we had never known.

When classes began in September, Bruno and I launched into one of the busiest periods of our lives. I was taking a double load of courses since most of the work would be a repetition of my earlier studies in Paris, at the Conservatory in Buenos Aires, and in St. Louis. I gave private lessons at the University for pay and Bruno and I were also teaching our private students back in the city. We had agreed this would be necessary for a time, but we didn't realize how hard it would be. We had arranged to have most of our classes in the mornings. Three days a week at noon we jumped into our car and drove the 60 miles to the city, taking Gustavo with us. On Saturdays we went in early in the morning. Between us we had to meet nearly 50 students in the city each week. Bruno would drop me off at one student's house, then drive to another in the same part of town. As soon as his lesson was over, he would pick me up, deliver me to the next house, and so on. It would have been difficult with just the two of us, but Gustavo complicated things still further. On most travel days we didn't get home until ten or eleven and we had to be up early for classes the next day.

In the fall of 1970 we celebrated our fifth anniversary in the United States and we immediately applied for citizenship. When it came through, in March 1971, we invited a large group of friends for a buffet supper in our honor. We are just as proud of our citizenship today as we were then. I am sad that so many natural-born citizens of this country don't recognize what a privilege it is.

I was now determined to start playing again in public, and began to do so at Sunday afternoon church recitals and occasional school assemblies. I learned right away that I had a long distance to go. The first of these recitals was probably the worst I have ever played. I forgot passages, stopped, picked up again and stumbled on. More than twenty times my memory betrayed me. Could anything be worth such a disastrous performance?

I was now studying with Martin Canin. He knew nothing about my medical history and I had decided not to tell him, still determined to succeed on my own without relying on others' sympathy. He was encouraging me to learn new music and I wanted to please him, learning new things just like any other student. In fact, I would never succeed unless I could perform new pieces. But my poor memory, overtaxed by all this new material, just revolted and refused to learn anything at all. I made a big mistake trying to pretend that my handicap didn't exist. If I had gone slower, learning fewer pieces and filling in with familiar ones, these recitals might not have been so discouraging.

Of course, another problem was that Bruno and I were trying to do a bit too much; so we decided to limit our trips to and from New York. Consequently we needed to get students in eastern Long Island. At first we advertised in local newspapers, but the ads brought few inquiries and fewer students. So we took matters into our own hands. Twice a week after dinner we propped Gustavo in the back seat of the car and drove around the neighborhoods leaving flyers in mailboxes. These brought us a few students and soon the new students brought us others. But I continued to teach at the University that second year even though I had completed my course work for a degree. In November I gave my required recital. It was a great improvement over my earlier appearances, but it wasn't good enough to satisfy Martin Canin. He couldn't understand why I kept having so much trouble with my coordination and why I seemed to forget music I'd had plenty of time to memorize.

By the end of the 1971–72 school year Bruno and I received our degrees. Now we would be able to select our students and not have to be nice to those with little interest and no ability.

That summer we visited the town in Italy where Bruno had been born. We visited six countries altogether and, of course, spent some time in Paris where I saw many of my old friends. Nadia Boulanger was now well into her eighties. Since the accident she had taken a special interest in me and I was delighted to see her again and to have Bruno meet her.

Our visit to Europe was particularly useful to Bruno. At Stony Brook he had been serving as assistant conductor of the university orchestra, as an assistant to composer Isaac Nemiroff teaching harmony, and on weekends as director of choral music at a Methodist Church in Setauket. In Europe, he had a chance to study at summer institutes and to conduct in summer festivals.

We returned to Stony Brook that fall in high spirits. Renewing old friendships in the international world of music reminded us that our calling was really beyond place. Wherever we were—Stony Brook, Buenos Aires, Paris— we had friends because music knows no boundaries.

When we got back from Europe I had reason to believe that I was pregnant, although I hadn't been sick a single day. I went back to my old friend Dr. de la Garza and asked him please to examine me. When he finished, he said, "Congratulations, you are fifteen weeks pregnant."

My feelings about having another child were somewhat complicated. On the one side, I felt that God ordained things like this and I looked forward to a second child to love and care for. But on the other, I had been so sick before Gustavo was born and the delivery had been so agonizing that I wasn't sure I could go through it again. The baby was due early in March.   179

That fall Bruno and I had nearly 150 private students a week. Now our students came to us and we didn't have to go to classes or drive to New York. For the first time since our marriage we were earning more money than we spent. I had time to practice on my own and was still playing several times a year in eastern Long Island. In fact, I was so encouraged by my progress that on one of our trips to the city that fall I went to see Norman Seaman, a concert producer, to inquire about arrangements for a recital in New York City.

But the new baby came first. As the due date came closer and closer, I found myself becoming more and more frightened. Dr. Pennisi, my gynecologist, kept trying to calm me, yet no matter what he said I was still frightened. Finally, on February 26, I went to see him for a regular checkup. The baby was due in only eight or nine days, but when he saw how scared I was he told me to check into the hospital the following day and he would induce labor.

Bruno and I stayed up most of the night getting things ready so that he and Gustavo could manage by themselves for a few days. The following morning I was admitted to the hospital. At 10 I was given an anaesthetic and at 1:02 in the afternoon our daughter Ana

Maria was born. As the doctor had predicted, the delivery was perfectly normal.

Later that same afternoon I called my mother in Buenos Aires. I felt wonderful. Ana Maria was born on a Tuesday, and Friday morning the doctor said I could leave the hospital if I would agree to stay off my feet a few days more. But I felt so good that on the way home I went shopping. People came up to ask how old the baby was and when I said seventy-two hours, they thought I was crazy.

On Sunday, I played the organ at church with Ana Maria lying in my lap. After the service several members of the congregation asked, "Weren't you pregnant last week?" I laughed and introduced them to Ana Maria.

Little Ana Maria started life the same way I had—in a crib near the piano where her mother was teaching all day. Now five, she already plays quite well and has the enthusiasm for learning that only a young, talented child can show. People have asked whether I will push her along into music as my mother did me. I can only answer yes.—I feel the responsibility to develop her talent. And yes, I shall push her if necessary.

Shortly after Ana Maria was born I asked Nadia Boulanger to be Ana Maria's godmother and she accepted. On April 22, Easter

Sunday, Ana Maria was baptized in New York with Mother standing in for Mlle. Boulanger. Ana Maria's godfather is the Rev. Father Jose Biain, a close friend of ours from Spain who has lived in the United States for many years.

♪ 27

NOT LONG after Ana Maria was born I talked to Martin Canin about playing a recital in New York. I had thought to rent Carnegie Recital Hall sometime during the next musical season. Mr. Canin liked Town Hall better and suggested I consider it instead.

I forgot about my discussion with Mr. Canin for a few months until one day in May when everything seemed to go wrong. Ana Maria cried half the day, my students weren't prepared, their parents were late paying. Enough, I said. Picking up the telephone I called Norman Seaman and told him that I wanted to set a date for a recital in Town Hall during the coming winter. He asked me to send a deposit of $600 and to come see him as soon as I had chosen a program.

Most casual music lovers think that if a performer is playing a concert in New York he or she is making money. Unfortunately, that's not true. Beginning performers have to *pay* large amounts of money to appear in a major 183 hall. They pay the regular rental fee for the hall, a commission to a concert manager and an additional sum to advertise the concert. In 99 cases out of 100, the tickets sold don't pay half the expenses. Only after a performer has become known through such appearances do bookings for paid concert work begin to arrive.

The concert date dispelled my gloom right away. I sat down and began to practice. All my life the prospect of a performance has made me cheerful and excited—at least until the date comes close. But soon I discovered that I was getting ahead of myself again. For my first recital in New York I had decided to play pieces that I had known for years. But when I sat down to play them, I realized how far I had to go. My full teaching schedule and the baby had kept me from practicing regularly. My coordination was lousy and the pieces sounded terrible. Summer was coming and we planned to visit Europe again. It just didn't seem possible that I could be ready by December or January. So I called Mr. Seaman and told him that I had decided to postpone my recital for a while.

The following spring Norman Seaman called. He said that it had been a year since he received my deposit and that he wouldn't 184 hold it for more than 18 months. If I didn't schedule a recital by the end of November I would lose my money. I asked him to give me a few days.

That night I sat down to play. I wasn't much better than I had been the year before. But the letter from my uncle reminding me that I was destined to become a performer had been much on my mind. If I'm not ready this year, when will I be ready? I asked myself.

The next day I called Mr. Seaman and told him to arrange a date. He had one already, he said—November 9, a Saturday, at 2 P.M.

I called Martin Canin. He was happy about the date and full of ideas about what I should play. After a few days' thought he suggested a beautiful group of pieces. There was only one problem—none of them were pieces I had learned before the accident, so I would have to memorize them all in my long difficult way. But I wanted to please him and loved the music he had chosen, so I agreed.

Summer came and we went to Europe again, but this time I felt guilty about not practicing. Of course I told myself that a vacation would be good for me, that it would leave me relaxed and ready to play. But I knew this wasn't true. A pianist is like an athlete: he or she must be in condition to play well. I was not in shape and should have been practicing every day just on this account. Also, I had a particular problem: if my memory didn't have plenty of time to learn the new pieces without pressure, it would forget them at the crucial moment. I resolved to begin practicing just as soon as we got home.

September is a terrible month for a teacher. Students and their parents call and visit continually to arrange the new schedule. Also Gustavo had to start school, the house needed cleaning, and Ana Maria, who was only eighteen months old, demanded my attention too. We had a few money problems as well; and I began to worry about the remaining $800 that we would soon have to pay Mr. Seaman for the concert. At the last moment Mrs. Rose Gordon, the mother of one of my best students at the Institute for the Blind offered to lend me the money for the Seaman organization. I accepted gratefully.

All at once it was the first week in October and there were only five weeks to go before the concert. Then came another shock. I had expected to practice eight hours a day for these last weeks, just as I had done all those years when I was younger. But I was so far out of shape that I could not practice nearly that long. After the first few days my fingers were raw and bleeding and my back was giving me trouble as well. So I had to slow down.

Norman Seaman called early in the month

to get a final program so that flyers could be prepared. Well, by then I knew that I would never be able to play Martin Canin's program —I had neither the time nor the energy to put it into performing shape and be sure of my memory. I told Seaman I would call him back. Then I called Martin Canin and tried to explain why I couldn't possibly play the program he had helped me select. Instead, I told him, I wanted to play the Beethoven "Appassionata" (which I had learned when I was 12), the Chopin "Grand Polonaise and Andante Spianato" (with which I had won a competition in Paris) , the B-flat-minor Scherzo by Chopin (which I had known since childhood), the piano sonata by Alberto Ginastera (an old favorite by my teacher in Argentina), and the "Piece for Piano" by Isaac Nemiroff, which he had dedicated to me when I was studying at Stony Brook. The last I would play with the music in front of me.

Mr. Canin wasn't at all pleased with this change of plan. The new program wasn't as well-constructed as the other, he protested, and critics might object to it. I answered that I would rather play a bad program well than a good one poorly. I wanted to explain why I *had* to play these particular pieces and why I was so frightened of playing in New York. But once again I held my tongue.

I'm sure Mr. Canin was expecting me to visit him for a final lesson before the recital. But with all the concert expenses, we were broke and I couldn't ask him to teach me for free. In late October, however, he called to say that he would like to hear my program. I explained our circumstances but he generously insisted on coming anyway. We settled on the following Monday. He would have a quick dinner with us, hear my pieces and stay overnight. Less than two weeks remained before the concert.

I played terribly for him that night. In three hours we got through only the Beethoven and the Chopin Polonaise. The worse I played the more nervous I got and the more my coordination and memory let me down. Though I wasn't as well prepared as I should have been, I didn't expect such a disaster. When I finished, Mr. Canin said, "Well, if you could practice 25 hours a day from now until the concert you might play fairly well."

The next morning after breakfast he left. saying he would be back the following Monday night—five days before the recital.

There were other disappointments that week. The piano in Town Hall was not particularly good. I asked how much it would cost to borrow one from Steinway, but the moving charges were more than I could pay. We also had no money for advertisements in the *Times* beyond the one or two Norman Seaman was responsible for. I began to worry that I would be playing a bad program on a poor piano to an empty hall. The Argentine consulate had offered to have a reception for "distinguished guests" after the recital—but how could we be sure that there would be any guests at all?

Though I kept up a full teaching schedule that week, I practiced every spare moment— late at night, early in the morning, at lunch.

On Monday, November 4, Martin Canin came again. After dinner we went to my studio and I played for him. It wasn't much better than the week before. He became very concerned and told me I shouldn't play the recital at all. When we rejoined Bruno our faces were so long that he too became concerned.

As Bruno poured the whisky, Mr. Canin began talking seriously. He wanted me to play well, but there was no way I could play well in only four days' time. "Losing your money is not nearly as important as losing your reputation," he said, "because you can't get your reputation back again."

I respected Martin Canin's judgment and this upset me. But there were some things I knew that he didn't. First, I had been on the stage all my life and I knew that when Saturday came I would play better. I always play well for an audience. Second, I had reached a stage in my life where I had to play a recital soon or never. I was afraid that if I canceled my date on November 9 I wouldn't ever have the courage to set another one. Of course he didn't know all the things that weighed on my mind—Dr. Rivadeau-Duma's advice, all those painful hours in Buenos Aires after the operation doing finger exercises on a closed keyboard, that awful moment after I'd played on the radio in La Plata when I realized I couldn't remember a single note of the piece I had just finished.

I tried to explain to him that I had to play. He felt the risk was too great and stood firm. Finally I began to cry. I didn't know what to do and I began to wonder whether I was just a fool for going through all this.

The last thing he said before we went to our beds stuck in my mind all the next week: "It is your life and your name. There is nothing I can do to stop you from playing. But if I were you I wouldn't play."

The next morning before he left he asked me to promise three things. First, to call him that afternoon after my rehearsal in Town Hall. Second, to cancel all my lessons for the week. And third, to practice every available minute between now and the concert. I promised, and asked him in return please to come backstage at Town Hall Saturday before I went on. I kept only two of the three promises. We could not afford to give up a week of my teaching income even for Town Hall.

✄ 28

THAT same morning Bruno and I drove in to the city with our good friends the Hahnkes, who were coming along to help my morale and to keep Bruno company. I had Town Hall from 10 to 1 that afternoon, but I scarcely cared. What difference would it make? Even the Hahnkes couldn't lift my spirits.

In those three hours I played through my whole program, but I don't believe I ever played worse in my life. Mistakes seemed to come every second and I pounded the piano in rage and despair.

After this I called Martin Canin as I had promised and told him that everything had gone as badly as the night before. Now that he knew I was going to play he didn't suggest I cancel. In fact, he was almost sympathetic—telling me, simply, to practice every minute of the last few days.

And practice I did, all the time telling myself that somehow everything was going to work out. But I still would wake up in the middle of the night in a cold sweat, trying to remember a certain passage and not being able to do so. As the days passed, and with them the week, it all began to seem like a bad nightmare. I was impatient with my students, impatient with Bruno and my children and worried about so many things. The dress I had bought didn't fit because I had gained weight. There was still no certainty there would be an audience. The piano worried me. And we were broke.

Finally Saturday came. As the hour approached I got more and more nervous.

Of course I had been to Town Hall earlier in the week, but then I was somewhat awed. Now, when we arrived on recital day, I saw how old and uncared-for everything was. In the dressing room programs for the previous night's concert were scattered around. The dressing room itself, above the stage, was dark and small.

I tried to relax, but I began to have the same fantasy that has come to me before every concert since the accident. First I get this overwhelming urge to run away and then I'm suddenly taking off on an airplane while the audience sits and waits. Fortunately Martin Canin then arrived to put me at ease.

Soon it was time for me to dress. And Beverly Rummel, a good friend from Stony Brook, was there to help. By the time I finished, Norman Seaman was outside to collect the final payment for the concert. Altogether, the recital cost $1400 not including my dress and certain extras. Ticket sales would cover part of this, but not a very big part.

As I sat at an upright piano in the offstage waiting room warming up, Mr. Canin and Mr. Seaman stayed with me and told each other jokes which I was in no mood to appreciate. At five minutes to two, Mr. Seaman told me that I should start at ten after. Then he wished me well and left. Mr. Canin left a moment later to take his seat.

Now there was only Beverly Rummel. We weren't talking, as I was trying to breathe regularly and slowly to gain a sense of calm. Then Bernie Hahnke rushed in saying that I must go on at once. The *Times* critic had just arrived and was likely to be angered if I started late.

When you walk out into the bright lights on a stage, your sense of time changes. Everything seems to happen in slow motion. The slightest delay takes an eternity, and the walk from the stage door to the piano seems as if it will never end.

But your mind is working much faster than

usual. I was mad at this critic I had never met who was rumored to be impatient and irritable. Of course I had no reason to be angry at him. But at moments of stress my own fright seems to turn into anger and I feel strong.

At last I arrived at the piano. Putting my hands in my lap I took a deep breath and said to myself a verse from the Bible that I have always remembered at such moments: "I can do all things through Him who strengthens me."

I raised my hands to begin Beethoven's "Appassionata" Sonata. On the very first page I missed the long run, beginning and ending on the wrong note. All at once Dr. Rivadeau-Duma's voice came up out of my past: "Don't . . . don't . . . don't." Martin Canin had said, "If I were you I wouldn't play." And somewhere out there was the *Times* critic waiting.

But then I thought of all those who had said, "You are a born musician." God had given me this talent not to be hidden away but to use! I thought of Monsignor Franceschi who had taught me so much about life. Germaine Pinault who had risked her own delicate health hour after hour, day after day, because she believed in me. My father with his courage. My mother with her prayers. And Bruno, now backstage, with his constant support. While out in the audience were Martin

Canin, my benefactor Mrs. Gordon, the Hahnkes, the Rummels and many more. These were my reasons for being here, and they would share in whatever success I had today.

I took a deep breath and closed my eyes, trying to conquer my fear and asking God's help. I had missed only one run; the recital was still in front of me. Then I concentrated on the music.

At the end of the "Appassionata" I took my bows and walked offstage. As soon as I was through the door, I said, "Water! Someone bring me water!" A hand reached out with a glass of iced water but my own hand was not steady. Before I could gain control of it the water spilled all the way down the inside of my dress. The shock was terrific and I just knew the stain would show. How could I go back out with the whole front of my dress wet? But miraculously it didn't show, and the shock took the edge off my nervousness.

After a careful drink from another glass of water, I returned to play Isaac Nemiroff's "Piece for Piano." Mr. Nemiroff was in the audience and, I later learned, he was as nervous as I. This was the New York premiere of his composition.

196   During intermission Martin Canin came

backstage. "The rest of the program is your stuff," he said, trying to keep me relaxed. And it was true. The Chopin and the Ginastera Sonata were favorites of mine.

I still ran into a few problems with Chopin's "Grand Polonaise," as my nerves simply would not let me relax. But during the Ginastera I played better and better both because I loved the music and because I knew the recital was nearly over. When I finished its rousing last movement, the audience cheered and many of them were on their feet. At last I could smile.

I had done it! Almost 13 years after the accident, after trials, false starts and many temptations to give up, I had finally made my New York debut. The nay-sayers, and particularly Dr. Rivadeau-Duma, had been proven wrong.

I knew the audience had been pleased, but what had the critics thought? As soon as I finished the last encore, I hurried backstage to look for Martin Canin. When I spotted him, I rushed to ask his impressions. Reminding me a little of Germaine Pinault, he said, "Not too bad." At first I was stung that he could find nothing more encouraging to say, but he is a perfectionist and that "not too bad" was actually quite positive for him. Maybe someday I shall play a recital that completely satisfies him. I hope so.

I had been told that a review in the New York *Times* would probably not appear until a week from that Sunday. So the next morning I was completely unprepared to see the headline:

MUSIC: ANA TRENCHI DE BOTTAZZI PLAYS

And just below that:

PIANIST IS IMPRESSIVE IN TOWN HALL RECITAL
HAS BIG TECHNIQUE AND USES IT WELL

The review was a good one and in no time Bruno and I were jumping all over the place. My performance and this review would allow me to continue playing. My career was safe, and I now felt that I could live fully once again.

29

AFTER the Town Hall success I wanted to go on a bigger stage, and after much consideration settled on Avery Fisher Hall, home of the New York Philharmonic Orchestra. This beautiful auditorium, built in the early 1960s, seats nearly 3000 people and is one of the pinnacles for a performing artist.

I reserved the auditorium for February 29, 1976, fifteen months after my Town Hall recital. Then I sat down to decide what to play. One evening when Bruno and I were discussing the new engagement, he pointed out that I had a much larger repertory than most performers. My years of study with Germaine Pinault had assured that. "You should offer to play any of fifty pieces," Bruno said, "and let the audience select what they want to hear."

At first the idea was only a joke. But the more I considered it the better it seemed. I knew that not one concert pianist in fifty would dare do such a thing. And even though nearly all the pieces would be ones I had learned before the accident, preparing to play so much from memory would test my mind in a way it had never been tested before. When I sat down to list the pieces I could play I found there were so many that we decided to offer a hundred instead. I also decided to disclose the facts about my accident and recovery.

It was inevitable that some people would regard the concert as simply a cheap parlor trick. But there were several good reasons to do it anyway. First, I knew that I could give performances of real musical substance, not just play-throughs. Second, offering 100 selections would attract some important publicity. For in the highly competitive world of New York concert performance, where scores of pianists perform every year, it is important to find some way to set yourself off from the rest. I didn't want to be a show-off, but I knew I didn't have the money or the time to give small-scale recitals until I was recognized.

Preparing for this recital was both fun and difficult. I enjoyed being able to practice everything—thirty-six hours of music altogether—rather than concentrating on four or five pieces. But as the recital date approached, I felt frustrated because I didn't know what to focus on.

The day of the recital I was a nervous

wreck. My mother had come up from Buenos Aires and I hadn't played with her in the audience for years. And, of course, I wouldn't know what I'd be playing until five minutes before I walked out on the stage.

For the last weeks I had the same nightmare every night. I was performing in Avery Fisher Hall for a large audience. But my left hand was playing one piece and my right hand another. The harder I tried to get them together, the worse it sounded until I woke up in a cold sweat.

At five minutes to three that afternoon— five minutes before concert time—the audience tabulators came backstage with the list of selections. I sat down and hurriedly put them in concert order. Then someone went out and announced the program to the audience:

Bach	"Jesu, Joy of Man's Desiring"
Beethoven	"Appassionata" Sonata
Chopin	Sonata in B-Minor

INTERMISSION

Chopin	"Minute Waltz"
	Waltz in C-Sharp Minor
Debussy	"Clair de Lune"
Ginastera	"Rondo on a Children's Theme"
Liszt	"Mephisto Waltz"

I was so nervous when I went on stage that I neglected to "picture" the first piece in my mind. I had played the beautiful Bach chorale many times and taught it to hundreds of students, yet I lost track of it on the third page. My left hand played a series of wrong notes as I realized that I didn't know what came next. This confusion lasted only a few seconds, and a moment later I picked up the thread of the music and played to the end with no more trouble. But I felt somewhat chastened.

The rest of the program went well, and I became increasingly pleased with myself. I *knew* I could do this and I was doing it. After the program ended I played an encore or two. Then I came out for one more, not even sure yet what I would play.

On the way to the piano I broke one of the oldest rules of performing. Instead of looking out just over the heads of the people in the last row, I looked down into the audience, and by chance saw Mother. Suddenly I felt a peculiar chill as I recalled the way she had forced me to practice when I was young. I could hear her voice saying, "Didn't I tell you you would be grateful someday? Didn't I tell you you would thank me for forcing you to practice?" All at once I was angry.

Early that morning she had managed to irritate me in the same way. "Don't play 'The Musical Snuff-Box,'" she had said. "I know you play it all the time, but I'm sick and tired of it." The piece had been one of my favorite encore numbers since I was a youngster and I had played it in Town Hall. But I had certainly not planned to play it that day.

Now as I sat at the piano, I smiled to myself and announced that I would like to play "The Musical Snuff-Box." It was my little way of getting even.

The recital was a musical success, but it had been frightfully expensive—nearly $8000. My Town Hall benefactor, Mrs. Gordon, had once more lent us the money and made the performance possible. As promising as things now seemed to be, I still needed an angel; and I was more grateful to her than I could say.

Having shown that I could play in public and having proved to myself that my mind could recall a huge quantity of music, it was time to break new ground. So I reserved Avery Fisher Hall for a third recital to be held in January 1977, and consulted Martin Canin about a program of new music—pieces I would learn for the occasion. This time I stuck to the program he helped me choose. I started with a charming eighteenth-century sonata by Galuppi and then played the difficult

"Wanderer Fantasy" by Schubert. The second half of the program was to include the Four Ballades by Chopin.

Three of the Ballades had special significance for me. The first I had learned as a child before leaving Argentina. The third I had learned with Germaine Pinault in twelve days for the competition at the Paris Conservatory when I was fifteen. And the fourth Ballade was the music I was listening to while driving through Belgium at the moment of my accident.

The fourth was the hardest to learn because of its associations. I knew the exact place in the piece—five lines from the end—when I hit the truck. For a long time I couldn't play past that spot. Approaching it, I would see the truck looming closer and closer, remember my panic and then the sickening impact of the crash. Only after playing through those bars time after time was I finally able to overcome these memories.

When I walked onto the stage that afternoon, I was astonished by the size of the audience. More than two-thirds of the 3000 seats were filled, and I made a mental note to thank all those who had helped publicize the event. Two men were especially important: Robert Jones, whose article on me had appeared in the New York *Daily News* that morning, and

Robert Sherman, on whose radio show I had recently appeared. I was particularly grateful for the crowd, too, for the sake of a new "angel," Dr. Helmuth Fuchs, without whose assistance I would not have been able to rent the hall.

The first half of the program went well. Then right in the middle of the first Ballade, I lost my picture of the music with no idea what should come next. The experience was as terrifying as ever, but this time my fingers kept playing! For moments on end I played as if by remote control, and through the rest of the Ballades I could "see" only fragments of the music. Then the concert was over—my third New York recital and a new benchmark.

Backstage after the last encore I first saw my friend Beverly Rummel with a big smile, and a moment later Martin Canin. I held my breath, waiting for his verdict and was overjoyed when he had just one word: "Bravo!"

Moments later, a very special visitor appeared. Mrs. Logan, had come all the way from Texas to hear me play. We embraced and both cried with happiness.

Late that night the first edition of the New York *Times* arrived at the newsstands. On the entertainment page a headline said, 205

That night I lay awake and marveled at my good fortune. I thought of all the people who had supported me, and of God, who had given me the strength to do so much more than medical science or plain common sense would ever have allowed.

❦ 30

THIS story, my story, began with "the accident," a decisive event in my life and one that has affected everything since.

But what is life, all life, except a series of accidents—not only disastrous ones, but good ones as well. It was an accident of sorts that I met Monsignor Franceschi and Germaine Pinault. If I had not been in Paris on vacation I should never have gone to Tokyo on three days' notice. Had I not felt homesick for my dog, I should not have met Bruno. And so on and so on. But I still believe that somewhere in all these events we call accidents the hand of God is at work.

One of the most interesting accidents that happens to all of us is our parents. We don't pick them, yet none of us can escape their influence. I have often been asked whether I would select another mother or father, and I say no. Alone, either one of them might have destroyed me. But together, with their very different ideas of love, they balanced each other. In their ways they were both harsh and gentle with me. And though they were not always kind to one another, the amazing thing is that in certain important ways they both agreed. Each taught me by words and example to dare and to never give up. Had I not been taught these things from the cradle, I should never have played again after the accident.

My battle isn't over. I have learned not to pretend that I have no handicap. Because when I do I get in trouble. The secret is to say "I have a handicap—but I am still a whole, full, human person." Most people use so little of their potential that I can still outperform them.

Often I'm asked, "How far can determination take a person?" And I answer with this example: If I decided that my goal was to become the first foreign-born woman president of the United States, it might take me twenty or thirty years, but I would make it. I am still working toward my real goals—to be an outstanding pianist, a good daughter, wife, mother, friend and human being—and I believe I will achieve them. How can I be so optimistic? I have my life to show.

Of course there are the uncertainties. Will my memory work today? Or is this a "clumsy day" when I will play as if my fingers are tied together? But even these uncertainties no longer depress me. Uncertainty is present in everyone's life; mine is just a particular kind. As long as I have life and health I will work toward becoming the best musician I can be.

There are still many things to do. Back during our darkest period in New York, Bruno and I dreamed of playing in Carnegie Hall together. I hope in the near future that dream will come true.

I know that I'm not wholly responsible for either my successes or my failures. God provides—He gives and He takes away. Mother once taught me a saying when I was a child: "What we are is God's gift to us; what we become is our gift to God."

I believe this. And to the extent that I use my talents, I succeed not just in achieving fame or recognition or satisfaction but in being able to look up to God and say, "This is my gift to You."